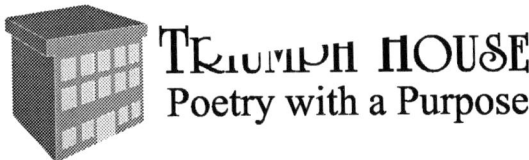
TRIUMPH HOUSE
Poetry with a Purpose

A BICYCLE MADE FOR TWO

Edited by

Neil Day

First published in Great Britain in 2001 by
TRIUMPH HOUSE
Remus House,
Coltsfoot Drive,
Peterborough, PE2 167
Telephone (01733) 898102

All Rights Reserved

Copyright Contributors 2001

HB ISBN 1 86161 974 X
SB ISBN 1 86161 979 0

FOREWORD

For many people poetry is a form of communication, used to express feelings to loved ones, family or friends.

This special anthology of creative poetry celebrates the gift of love in all its many guises, as each author shares their heartfelt feelings for others with you, the reader. Memories are the most valuable and emotive attributes that a person possesses. Even the memory of a glowing sunset or the love of one particular person can be something we will treasure for all time.

The subject of love varies greatly from poem to poem, be it for a partner, family member, friend or even just a love of life in general.

This unique anthology is sure to entertain, this is a truly inspiring collection to be read time and time again.

Neil Day
Editor

CONTENTS

My Shadow	Dora Watkins	1
Two Peas In A Pod	Zeedy Thompson	2
Whilst You Are Away	John L Pierrepont	4
Bella's Game	Les Merton	5
Midnight Painting	H Val Horsfall	6
Lonely Tom	T A Napper	7
Love Of My Life	Irene Hanson	8
Soul Mates	Bridie Bonello	9
Soul Mates	Gina Millet-Rivera	10
He	Nicky Young	11
My Joy	V M McKinley	12
Two Friends I Once Knew	M Cowan	13
Opposites Attract	S Mullinger	14
You	G Poole	15
With Love To You I Write This	Don Woods	16
Donald	Daphne Baker	17
When You've Gone	Suzi Vanderborght	18
Soul Mates	Pamela Di Nicoli	19
Someone Special	Linda Kettle	20
Kisses	S H Smith	21
One Of Life's Heroines	Angie Scarth	22
Soft Soap	Barbara Williams	23
Till Tomorrow	Eduardo Del-Rio Escalona	24
Special K	Michael Bellerby	26
Living In Me	Dan Pugh	27
True Love	Jess Chambers	28
Without You	Margaret Findlay	29
Golden Age	Margaret Marsh	30
Invisible Girl	Tina Watkin	31
A Special Friend Remembered	Amanda Jayne Biro	32
A Sunny Little Prayer	Paul Holland	33
Discovery	Brenda Dove	34
Ode To Mo	Mike Monaghan	35
Still Life	Sally Spedding	36
Recordings	Roger Thornton	37
Golden Love	J M Judd	38

Our Vows	Jacqueline Farrell	39
What Loving Is For	David Whitney	40
Living Is To Love And Love Is Living	Joan E Blissett	41
Her Face In Autumn	Paul Willis	42
Love Takes Wing	Marian Lacy	43
A Mother's Love	Colette Breeze	44
Summer Of Love	N Callear	45
Summer of 1978	H G Griffiths	46
The French Poetess	Pam Cook	47
To Louise	A J Vogel	48
October Wisdom	Pamela Constantine	49
True Romance	Reg Summerfield	50
Love Is	Barbara Ellison	51
Why	Julie Brown	52
David And Bathsheba	D Hendtlass	53
The Heights	Philip Burton	54
A Love Poem	Keith Johns	55
I Just Wanted You	Rosaleen O'Brien	56
Impression	Alan Holdsworth	57
You Are	Ron Marland	58
Midsummer Yearning	Dorothy	59
Love Is A Circle	Anne de Menezes	60
Statue Of Love	Frank Howarth-Hynes	61
The Wedding Anniversary	Eric Allday	62
A Song To Remind Me	Haidee Williams	63
Visibly Affected	Gareth Wynne Richards	64
Love Is	Leslie Holgate	65
Each Day	Amanda Steel	66
Summer Roadside Rose	Jennifer M Trodd	67
Where Did True Love Go?	Mary Miller	68
Young Love	Linda Ann Marriott	69
Baby Brother	Parveen Kaur Saini	70
The Dark Ocean	Craig Shuttleworth	71
Romantic Thoughts At Eventide	Hazel Vambria Walters	72
Thoughts About Love In Our 50th Year Of Marriage	Ian Purvis	73

Miss Right? One's Troth To Plight? Maybe!	Dennis Overton	74
My Cat Sandy	Helen E Schofield	76
Here And There	Jeanette Gaffney	77
Beach Girl	David Russell	78
Oh My Love	W T Stringfellow	79
Solstice In The Glade	Andrew Whitfield	80
Love Where Have You Gone?	Nicky Young	81
Rebound	Pauline Smith	82
My Hysterectomy	Mary Hudson	83
One Man	Kim Montia	84
Unrequited	Gemma Guymer	85
Summer Of Love?	Paul A Reeves	86
Resolution	S H Smith	87
My First Love - 1943	J H Van Grinsven	88
Don't You Find It Strange?	Jim Sargant	89
To My Dearest Love	Anthony Manville	90
I Love You, David	Margaret A Greenhalgh	91
Summer Dance	Katrina Shepherd	92
Wildlife Armageddon	Peter Morriss	93
The Woman At The Well	Jean Hazell	94
Guessing	Mary Tickle	96
Connected	Lee Walford	97
Summer Daze	Betty Lightfoot	98
Summer's Birth	John Christopher	99
The Sea	Sara Newby	100
Green Fingers	D J Price	101
God Provides - We Enjoy	Beryl Lenihan	102
Ode To Nightfall	Joan Lewington	103
Midsummer Foxgloves	Penelope Freeston	104
Changes	Cathy Mearman	105
After Winter	Margaret Carter	106
Summer Day	Joy Jenkins	107
First Light	Ann G Wallace	108
Inside, Looking Out	Pat Heppel	109
Basic Orientation	Brian Bates	110
Apocalypse	Carl Kemper	111
Gulf Coast Sunset	Ray Ryan	112

The Big Flood	G Morrisey	113
Life Of The Seeds	Sharon Joy Wandless	114
Stop	A Bhambra	115
Through The Window At My World	Janet Kelly	116
Concrete Home	Steve Pape	117
Never Too Old To Learn	R Grainger	118
Brunch	Peter Asher	119
Big Shot!	Hilary Jill Robson	120
The Zoo	Edith Antrobus	122
Christmas Night	Joyce M Turner	123
Teachings	Cathrine Campbell Rodgers	124
The Lesson	Jean Gray	125
No Longer A Joke	Kevin Challis	126
Book Of Life	Patricia Spencer	127
Missing You	Nicola Barnes	128
A Soft Touch	Anita Richards	129
The Plan Is	F McFaul	130
A Journey To Reality	Matthew L Burns	131
Happiness	Joan Sansom	132
My Offering	Ann S Clifton	133
Share A Prayer	Anne Macleod	134
Just Out Of Reach	Cynthia Smith	135
Relax Me Lord	Sandra J Walker	136
Holding My Hand	Pat Bidmead	137
The Word	Kathleen Dodd	138
Dear God	Marjorie Wagg	139
Loading Up	Frank Keetley	140
A Day At The Beach	Mick Rose	141
Anytime, Anywhere	Ian Caughey	142
Memory-Kept Kisses	D P R Stockton	144
. . . And Jesus Spoke!	Andrew Duncan	145
Life Wasn't Always Like This	Meg Bremner	146
Poetry	Joseph Broadley	147
To A Muse	Jeanette Latta	148
Memories Of Northlands	A H Thomson	149
Evacuation Of The Cities, September 1939	Doreen Dean	150

The Hobble Gobble Man	Barbara Tyers	151
Hoax No Joke	Joyce Clegg	152
The Grimgin Man	Julie Ann Evans	153
Cartier Cat	Jane Taylor	154
So I Am Black	Rosemary C Whatling	155
Pestilent Doors	Simon Morton	156
1984-1999	J Noble	157
Hangman's Noose	Eunice Neale	158
Who Walked Before	Keith L Powell	159
The Old Cemetery	L Brooks	160
Days Out	Mark Lloyd	161
If I Could Be	Pamela Coope	162
Yearning!	A E Garrod	163
Red	Peter de Dee	164

MY SHADOW

I have got a little shadow
That is now my other self
He always keeps his eye on me
Since he took me off the shelf
He is ever so protective
Yet he gives me a free rein
Knows with confident conviction,
That I will come back again
He is my Jack and I'm his Jill
We'll not fall down any hill
We'll make a heaven of our home
Then end up Darby and Joan.

Dora Watkins

TWO PEAS IN A POD

My heart delights in rapture at your devotion,
You set my desires soaring with your dedication,
Your presence asserts, you're like a pearl
A little clumsy but darling you are my girl.

You give me inspiration, you make my heart dance
With such adoration uplifting, I'm in a trance.
How can I live without you, my garden of fine hue?
You've renewed my life never again will I be blue.

I've loved you since the day of your birth
Now you've given me pleasure beyond measure
I wish you could stay this young for ever and ever
But time marches on, age respects no one person
So joy is resplendent in a clover for all seasons.

I grant you happiness and because you're clever
Your ambitions without inhibition I discover
You are soft and light my admirable granddaughter
Nurturing a smile in profusion like a heather
You're the feather in my cap I love and admire.

You relate to the humble with no motion to grumble
A scope for relationship all concerned can handle
Understanding and patience are sources to merit
The close family resemblance you inherit
Gives me assurance to support our association.

Such pleasure I derive when your presence is near
Is as high as a mountain because you're dear
The apple of my eye, joys of my delight
Prudence achieved, my morning of light.
Your embrace is enchanting, your smile disarming.

Your voice soft and gentle
Your love the greatest mantle
Moderation can gather
Enclosing us together
Like two peas in a pod.

Zeedy Thompson

WHILST YOU ARE AWAY

Whilst you are away, I miss you so much
My daily life is such and such
When you are here, I have a routine
Always knowing you will be seen.

Calling to ask for advice or to tell
Whether you're happy, or going through hell
The life you have chosen will never be right
Away from me, and out of my sight.

At this moment of time
You are in a foreign clime
But you managed to call
To tell me you're fine.

I loved the thought that you had to call
I know you had not forgotten me at all
Me here at home, thinking always about you
You overseas, but never doubtful.

I hope in your heart, you wished I was with you,
Always attentive, to help and to give you,
My love, my devotion, no matter where
I'm still here you're over there.

It will not be long, before you are back
To your routine, back on track.
In the meanwhile, I'm all alone,
You far away, me here at home.

You know I will always be here for you,
I hoping you are, the same for me,
Back to our chatter and laughter
Both together, now and here after.

John L Pierrepont

BELLA'S GAME

Bella's doorstep welcome kiss
was worth waiting for, perhaps,
it was for a neighbour's benefit.

We settled on her lounge sofa,
Bella's opening gambit,
'It's time we had a little drink.'

Wine and conversation flowed,
compliments filtered cigarette smoke
with an age old stratagem of modesty

inviting accidental touching.
Eyes meeting over wine glasses
encouraged flattering kisses.

A subtly introduced second bottle
encouraged a middle game
of soft lights and love songs.

Dancing was compulsory,
although the steps were unsteady
they still passed for a smooch.

'It's getting late.' Preceded
Bella's one for the road. Black coffee,
laced with a liberal dash of brandy.

This farewell ritual was repeated
several times to end with,
Bella's end game manoeuvre.

*'You'd better stay, the spare bed is made.
You'll have plenty of room, it's a double.*

'Check and mate Bella.'

Les Merton

MIDNIGHT PAINTING

I would use stars, a million stars,
To paint the dimly moonlit sky;
And ring it round with bright haloes
Of comets slowly drifting by;
Etch with silver, blue horizons;
Highlight with gold the flashing blue;
Tint green the trees that hold the sky;
I'd surely paint them all for you.

H Val Horsfall

LONELY TOM

A lonely, miserable widower, lost and so forlorn
Took in a rescued terrier, which gave him a brand new dawn.

He called it Bob, soon they were pals, they were together every day.
Now all his days were sunny when they had been so grey.

Then along came a widow lady, his romantic memory to jog,
She loved to help and do for him but did not love the dog.

A conflict in the widower's life, what would come to pass?
The dog knew that she hated him and one day nearly bit her arse.

This was to be the final straw between the two loves of his life,
Did he want the terrier or a prospective wife?

A problem so vexed but the living have to live,
Both pet and prospective partner had so much to give.

So he built a very plush dog kennel and an ample run,
The lady reluctantly would tend the dog at meal times,
          So a relationship had begun.

Bob was getting used to her, she bought him nice things to eat
And when relaxing in the garden, he would lay across her feet.

Sadly suddenly she was left alone, the time that we all dread,
Guess who never leaves her side, and sleeps across her bed?

T A Napper

LOVE OF MY LIFE

I love you every morning
I love you every night
I love you every minute dear
And I love you to hold me tight
I want you all the time dear
I want you close to me
I want your warm embraces
And I want to kiss you endlessly
For you are the love of my life dear
You are the man that I adore
I could never leave you
Because you are my amour.

Irene Hanson

SOUL MATES
(For Loopy)

It's our place, here, beneath this birch
Whose leaves give dappled shade,
Upon our backs we gaze up to the sea,
Pass tranquil time together
Exchanging childhood memories
At peace within each other's company.

We take our lunch and picnic
Side by side upon your rug,
And no one really knows just where we are,
Sitting here, beneath the sunshine
Golden moments passed in unison
Together, here, in perfect harmony.

We listen to the silence,
Discuss our hopes and fears,
Surrounded by our forest and alone;
With birdsong on the breeze
Wish this moment was infinity,
Within our dreams we are forever free.

When our time of passing comes
Perhaps our folks will find
A quiet spot beneath an oak
To place us side by side . . .
Two friends who loved the forest,
Now resting, soul mates in the sun.

Bridie Bonello

SOUL MATES

From the very first time I saw his face
It felt like peaches and cream, satin and lace,
Everything about it felt so right
When I looked into his eyes it was love at first sight.

At that moment the sun began to shine,
Summer had started and all was fine,
Even our faces were aglow with delight
That very first meeting on a hot summer's night.

Six years later and love is still strong,
When he takes me in his arms nothing can go wrong,
When he leaves for work each day,
A kiss and a hug and I love you he will say.

He is my soul mate that's for sure,
Sending music to my heart an instant cure,
When he is near me my soul begins to glow,
Knowing in my heart he will never go.

Gina Millet-Rivera

HE

I really feel it would not be wise,
My opposite sex to criticise.
For our God, our Creator was He,
And Jesus His Son, who set us free.

God made each and every man,
In His own image – His perfect plan.
God made man as one to be at His side,
He made woman for man to guide.

Love and kindness did God also create,
His plan was not for man to hate.
But He like Himself – humble at heart,
And loving words to impart.

So when I love the one opposite to me,
Within my soul I expect him to be.
My strength, my help, my loving friend,
At one with God till the very end.

Nicky Young

MY JOY
(Dedicated to Matthew - My grandson)

You set my words to music
To a tune that's all your own.
Your imperfect lips are smiling
To perfection,
        For me alone.

Wrapping your arms around me
You kiss my wrinkled cheek
You whisper 'I love you Nana'
And it's impossible,
        To speak.

You light my world with wonder
My love for you is deep.
You make me feel so very proud
With happiness,
        I weep.

My memories are so lovely
You're my inspiration, my joy
My future is full of light and love
Because of you my dear,
        Sweet boy.

V M McKinley

TWO FRIENDS I ONCE KNEW

Two friends I once knew went everywhere together:
You really would have said they were birds of a feather.
But peas in a pod just didn't seem to fit,
They were the long and the short of it.
Four foot ten and five foot eight,
But neither could have found a better mate.

M Cowan

OPPOSITES ATTRACT

You're loud and brash, so different to me,
But without you, wherever would I be?
I'm neurotic, worrier that's for sure,
But a hug from you works well as a cure.

If I'm tearful, you really are patient,
But when I am happy, then you're content.
Sometimes I know I drive you to despair,
But you'll not desert me, because you care.

S Mullinger

You

You fill my life
  You light my sun,
You make me feel
  Life has begun,
-   With you.

You light my eyes
  You lift my heart,
You make me feel
  That I'm a part
-   Of you.

You make me laugh
  You make me sigh,
You make me feel
  That I would die,
-   For you.

G Poole

WITH LOVE TO YOU I WRITE THIS

With love to you I write this
And from my heart these words I say
Your love and understanding
Are what makes each brand new day

Your hand on mine, your gentle smile
From lips so soft and warm
Your eyes reflecting all that's good
All bring the sun each morn

My darling life for me would end
Should you decide to leave
Without you standing at my side
Each day and night I'd grieve

So take and hold this love I give
Hold it captive in your heart
And we'll walk life's road together
And know peace at each day's start

Don Woods

DONALD

Who will worship
The ground I tread
Though flights of fancy
Fill my head?
Who'll squeeze my hand
And laugh with me
Whilst bringing me down
To reality?
Who will read me
Like a book
And know my secrets
With a look?
Encourage me
And with me go,
Lift my spirits when I'm low?

Your smile, those eyes,
Your gentleness,
Your spirit's still there
With me – I guess.

Daphne Baker

WHEN YOU'VE GONE

My toothbrush looks so lonely,
Where *your* brush once stood so tall.
No shaving foam around the sink,
Or shavings up the wall.

The toothpaste tube still has its lid,
And neatly squeezed up tight,
No toenail clippings in the bath,
And the tap won't drip tonight.

Familiar smells, and sights and sounds,
Undies on the floor.
Toilet lids are never shut,
Wet towels draped on the door.

For all the little irritants,
(Your habits drive me mad!)
But when your presence can't be felt,
Strangely I feel sad.

Suzi Vanderborght

SOUL MATES

Together for fifty years
Of loving joy and tears
Much that made us glad
Times when we were sad
And I would do my best
To put your mind at rest

You liked to be outdoors
So we tramped the moors
And sat on purple heather
Just happy when together
We'd wend our way along
Singing a favourite song

In the autumn of your life
You'd turn to me your wife
Caring for your every need
To be with me you'd plead
I stayed close by your side
Until the day that you died

Memories pass the time away
But I miss you more each day
This morning the sun shone
I can't believe you are gone
And in the garden I walked
Where often we had talked

We loved to hear you sing
And make the rafters ring
A gifted voice we thought
To win the fame you sought
Now forever my shining star
Guiding me from heaven afar

Pamela Di Nicoli

SOMEONE SPECIAL

You never took me in your arms
And made me your lover
It went deeper than that,
A joining of minds
A union of hearts, two halves
Separate without the other.

There was a moment when time
Meant nothing, and nothing
So important as being together
Breathing the same air,
The hours fell away till there
Was only the present, only today.

I felt cherished and special
For the person I was,
Not the one I would become
Shaped by the past
And moulded to someone's future
Measuring up like the total of a sum.

You rejoiced in me and I in you
Charged with a fondness that
Grew from the instant we met,
And in the short time our paths entwined
I have enough memories
To fill the darkest corners of my mind.

I always understood your thoughts
The words you left unsaid,
We spoke the same language
Shared the same past, it reminds me
Of something I once read:
Friendship goes deeper than romance – it lasts.

Linda Kettle

KISSES

Your kisses, sweeter than the choicest wine,
Have showered upon me like an autumn rain;
And I would render back what would be mine,
If only to receive them once again.
For in receiving, there is my delight –
To drink, and drink again their golden store,
And never would I pause but to requite
Myself in you, and boldly ask for more –
Until, inebriated with your breath,
And perfumed with its fragrance as a flower,
I would be glad to seal my bliss in death,
And make a heaven of this immortal hour.
So do I dream – that long before I wake,
You drain yourself of kisses for my sake.

S H Smith

ONE OF LIFE'S HEROINES

She is one of the heroines
Sweeping emphatically up and down the cobbled streets of my life
Patiently supporting me up the slanting highways and slipways
Always laughing
When pushchair wheels stick in the ruts
She always arrives smiling and breathless shifting shopping bags
From hand to hand and always finding the time for a hug

As noisy children we shrieked at the school gates there's
Russell's mum and Ian's mum and here comes Sharon's dad's
New wife, but
There's my mummy waiting
She waves with hands scarred by groceries and too much washing up
Laughing as she catches the echoes, as we rush by,
Of all the old childhood songs

After school
Bread and butter and jam and always newly baked cakes
She does the house and sweeps the floor and cleans the furniture and
Up and down and up and down
The cobbles streets and then
After Dad is settled and fed and I am asleep she joins Russell's mum
Across the cobbled streets running
To avoid the rain she runs between the drops and meets
Ian's mum and Sharon's dad's new wife
And then only then she is a wild woman, a girl with secrets, a seducing
temptress, a bohemian painter, a famous film star, a writer
Of history books
She plots her life and dreams

A native captive rising from the ashes of domestic chaos
Just like a heroine should.

Angie Scarth

SOFT SOAP

I used to look forward with pleasure
To watching my favourite Soap
A few precious moments of leisure
An escape to a world of hope
A chance to relax and unwind
With dreams that might never come true
Nothing cruel or even unkind
Explore social issues elsewhere
Let entertainment be the aim
Escapism - be that as it may
It helped a tired housewife
Relax at the end of a day
Make believe now seems forbidden
Storylines dire and sad
All with a tortured ending
Alike as peas in a pod
Each episode full of foreboding
Couples must be lesbian or gay
Children with behavioural problems
Or a sad killing along the way
Someone with terminal illness
Or an unwanted pregnancy
It makes it all depressing
A similar theme for each plot
Why not put all agonising together
And have just one Soap for the lot

Barbara Williams

TILL TOMORROW

It has been just a few days Papá, since I heard your voice tremble
. . . Tired it seemed to me, over the phone line and distance
While we talked casually of things without much importance

And as the words were back and forth, I could perceive your fatigue
You were trying not to worry me, as the loving father you have always
Been, and in a sigh of love, you were making me realise . . .
That you were frail, dearest Papá, and probably we wouldn't see each
Other no longer on this earth, but soon in paradise land.

I know that you believed me Papá, when I told you once at home
That our inheritance, wasn't only of this world that we can see
And that our souls have been travelling, for the cycles of the
Centuries, Amen.

From my sister today I learned, that at the break of dawn . . .
As usual you left your bed . . . but this time, in a last farewell,
Looking through the window, to the world you were leaving behind

I also know what else you were evoking at the edge of your departure
Besides your distant seeds and the most precious; your wife . . .
The love for those mountains, valleys, rivers, and ravines . . .
That were the green crystal carpet, to the beauty of younger days

You cut the rope of this life with the bravery of a warrior
Who is ready for his journey and the conquering of new frontiers
Where he is willing to go, in soundless silence and no goodbyes

My sorrows have no end, adored, beloved Papá . . .
'Cause I wasn't there, at your side, in that glorious final moment
I would have loved to soften your way, as you did when I was born

For you I have died twice, in silent pledge that now I'm offering
It will be my oath of loyalty to you, and I will sow my body . . .
In your green emerald of the south, waiting to reunite forever
. . . With the invincibility of your soul

I remember when you told me, that in a night of gusting winds
That were making their way puffing, through windows, roofs
                                                      and bindweeds
The voice of my grandma came, to give you her last farewell
                                                      and concern
To see my mother's pain and to keep her safe and sane

For fifty-six years you did that, and much much more Papá
And tonight like that unique night, I'll be waiting for your voice
To comfort me with your stories, because I need you so much

From distant heavens I see, advancing legion of a thousand colours
Swooping . . . hurling to pay their respect to your honourable life

Opening the skies for you, they point the way to your happiness
Where in universal love . . . at the end of my days
I will soar from this realm, to embrace you forever more

Fly my dear Papá . . . fly spreading your light
Because the light of your soul, is the sparkle of my now orphaned one
That's why I need to see you tomorrow . . . in the house of the
                                                          Eternal God.

Eduardo Del-Rio Escalona

SPECIAL K

You are my solid bedrock foundation
And I love for you total admiration
You have been my shining light
And helped me in my plight
Your smile is like the sun
My race is all but won
Never ever leave me
Say it will never be
The things you do
Mean I love you
Please take care
Don't despair
You're mine
For all time
We're here
It's clear
That
We
R
Forever
Together
Never part
Lonely heart
We two are one
It's so much fun
I know you're there
Life's not always fair
But standing by my side
My feelings I won't hide
I see brighter things ahead
Like those I've always said
My very life is in your hands
I'd give my all to your demands
So could you love me all your life
My lovely sweet and charming wife
And if my lover we should ever part
That would positively break my heart.

Michael Bellerby

LIVING IN ME

Smile that gentle smile;
Let your blue eyes dance and laugh
As they used to do . . .
Let yourself go for a while,
And enjoy your life again.

Come along with me
And listen to birds singing
In leafy hedges;
Feel cool grass caress your feet
While your shoes swing from your hand.

Dance among the stars
And sing love songs to the moon;
Stay with me 'til dawn
And drift into wonderland -
Minds and bodies intertwined.

Come and share my life
As you did when we were young,
And all our future
Was a gold road to take us
Into Heaven together.

Destined forever
To be we two together
And never to part,
You will always live in me,
At the centre of my heart.

Dan Pugh

TRUE LOVE

'I love you,' he said
As he held her tight,
Many years ago
On their wedding night.

'I love you,' he said
As he gazed with pride
On mother and babe
Lying side by side.

Closer they grew
As the years drifted by.
'I love you,' he whispered
His last dying sigh.

Jess Chambers

WITHOUT YOU

What will I do when you're not there,
My world will be no longer fair,
Each hour will feel just like years,
And I will shed a million tears.

You will be missing from your chair,
There will be no footstep on the stair,
No longer hear you call my name,
Our little house won't feel the same.

Holidays will be so dull for me,
No strolls along the beach and sea,
Music won't make me want to dance,
Sad my days with no romance.

Now I can only hope and pray,
That in Heaven we'll meet one day,
I'm thankful for our love so sweet,
For you have made it so complete.

Margaret Findlay

Golden Age

A youth passed by my window back in the days of yore
    His working life about to start, his school days gone before;
Nice an' handy with a spanner as each day he sweated and toiled
    To see that all machinery was run on wheels well-oiled.

But as the years rolled slowly by he swapped his set of spanners
    For a desk and phone and typist, cups of tea and office manners
He's adamant and stubborn, he wants this and that amending,
    Yet sometimes quite considerate with gratitude unending.

And now he's reached the golden age his work is never done
    Making sure that all the factory on well-oiled wheels is run;
Who passes by my window as I'm typing week by week,
    Sure, my youth back in the days of yore, my husband boss unique.

Margaret Marsh

INVISIBLE GIRL

I know I am invisible
People seeing straight through me.
A total nonentity
Is what I seem to be.

The world, it quite walks past me
As though I am not there;
As I reach out helping others
They seem almost unaware.

Side-stepped by many races;
Unseen as I drift by.
Overlooked by many faces;
Unheard my silent cry.

Alone in crowded places,
I'm blending with the wall;
Whilst lists of names are uttered
It's not my name they call.

I've noticed on occasions
When groups of friends I meet,
I am the one who always tends
To 'find' no vacant seat.

The only recognition
As I turn to dim the light,
My mirror's own reflection
Fondly wishes me 'Goodnight'.

Tina Watkin

A SPECIAL FRIEND REMEMBERED
(Kelsa 1992-2001)

I said my goodbyes,
As I watched you die.
My special friend,
I loved you until the end.

Wished you could have stayed,
For just another day.
To be by my side,
With dignity and pride.

The joy I'll always treasure,
Within endless moments of pleasure.
That keep your spirit alive,
Within your determination and drive.

You gave me a love so divine,
That it will always be mine.
For my heart to keep,
Like a dream as I sleep.

That takes me to your shore,
Within times we shared before.
Now memories of the heart,
That will never depart.

Amanda Jayne Biro

A Sunny Little Prayer

A tranquil light in your heart, the star that guides . . .
Love is a ray of sunshine, you send a friend . . .
Missing their loved presence -
Never diminishes the love you have for someone, or wish them -
Even if they love another, that's okay -
You still love and care for them from in your heart,
That never changes.
Some things come into our hearts,
There, never to be removed - by crowbar,
Dynamite, or maybe not even a supernova!
The memory of their smile, the truth of their kindness -
All the kinds of beautiful they are to you,
Always illuminates your heart . . .
Faith in love . . . sustains!
The love of a friendship, kindred to sunlight, a true warmth,
Always there . . .
However far friends loved are!

Paul Holland

DISCOVERY

Will you tell me of your body?
Will you take my hand and dance
Quiveringly over compliant flesh?
Muscles straining at the leash
Contours of perfection peaked
Ruby nipples stand erect
I admire in urgent need
Of you - entering me
On silken thrusts of rhythm
Moist mouthings orchestrate
Until replete
We separate
Intimately.

Brenda Dove

ODE TO MO
(Maureen)

Wish you were here, wish I was there,
in our yearning for completeness to become one as a pair,
I find you in my thoughts every place I go,
as in bygone days of yesterdays I love you my dearest Mo.
Maybe our love is like the universe, full of mystery that intrigues
                                                                                the brain,
or sitting at a blazing fire, when winter's outside unleashing
                                                                                 snow or even rain.
When our hearts become heavy, we both want to be alone
then memories of our love ignite and we seek somewhere to call
                                                                                    our home.
Sometimes I know we feel like letting go,
then our spirits acting as one answer a clear definitive no.
Maybe our love is snuggling close together,
just to have dreams of sunlit flowers, moonstruck rivers, stars
                                                         hovering above in cloudless weather.
If only we could be one forever more all our dreams would come true,
the marriage of our pure love would be, *you for me and*
                                                                        me for only you.

Mike Monaghan

STILL LIFE

Not Cana, this, but England's heart
Where horses stand close by in dappled
Shade. Where foxgloves and delphiniums
Plucked and cut to size now strain for the
Wild places. While through the meadow,
Sweat already celebrating on their skin,
Forges the tribe of wilderness . . .

Not Isaac and Rebekah, this, but a glowing
Gypsy queen of ivory and bronze. From Wales?
Iberia? Who knows? For her hair is host to
A myriad of stars borrowed from the night . . .

'I will,' each says in turn then summons God
To bless as the field beyond the temple moves
On His breath, the whispers of yesterday, tomorrow
Holding the children to its secrets. Tag and make
Believe, while on the steps, confetti comes,
Translucent in the heady sun. Lifting, falling as
The ink dries in the book and the horses
Nudge their way into the light.

Four chairs now perch amongst the summer's
Grass. An incongruity of gold and blue, souvenirs
Of laughter, music. Slight as brittle bones in
The early silence . . .

Sally Spedding

RECORDINGS

There they make mistakes over times struck matches
There love lies forlorn in the dead of night
Waiting for his reaches

It had been a sad song repeated in every line
Awaiting his touch while swans move into place
And make love in the broadness of the river

While ripples make recordings in the lake of past
Summer romances and fall into place
At the call of his music to its daily sounds.

Roger Thornton

GOLDEN LOVE

Do you remember,
The days gone by,
When in the grass,
Together we'd lie.

The sun always shone,
Or so it may seem,
Every day passed,
In a golden dream.

Loving was easy,
When we were young,
We'd laugh and kiss,
Under the sun.

But now we are older,
Now that we know,
How good it was,
So long ago.

J M Judd

OUR VOWS

People's voices are all in whisper,
   Organ music is playing low,
All dressed up in Sunday best,
   Nowhere else to go.

They're all waiting for somebody
   To appear at the door,
Soon they will appear there,
   Do you know what for?

Today there is a wedding,
   People start all to sing,
So the groom and bride today,
   Will exchange a ring.

Then at the reception,
   They both dance merrily,
Off now on their honeymoon,
   Together, happy we will be.

Jacqueline Farrell

WHAT LOVING IS FOR

An ache like no other,
A yearning to touch
The love of another,
You love oh! so much
A sigh of emotion,
The hush of the night
The dreaming, the wonder
Lost, praying for light
A memory's kiss,
That no one can compare
The part of me missing
When you're gone and not there
My tears barely drying,
Fore others appear
My eyes stung with crying
For wanting you near
My arms lost with nothing
Too precious to hold
A heart scarcely beating
From feeling the cold
Till last comes your perfume
And daring to stare
Your smile and your being
Is waiting right there
And rushed with my feelings
I burst with delight
And kiss you and hold you
Just ever so tight
For without you I'm nothing
A man and no more
But you've shown me love
And what loving is for.

David Whitney

LIVING IS TO LOVE AND LOVE IS LIVING

And love has landed me
On the pinnacle of life.
Our love is a singular pleasure,
Pure and sweet.
No sour discord will ever
Push aside the harmony
We hold beneath our feet.
No petty intrusion
Into our love
Will last as long as love
And love can hold.
It leaves its mark
And in so doing
Frowns upon the cynics.
Its power and protrusion
Glimmers and gleams
Its way into your whole,
Your very soul.
The sadness of a lost love
Can increase the quality of your life.
Just hold the meaning
Deep inside,
Remove the hurt
And leave behind the beauty
That love can give,
And use your love
To nurture love
And live to love for love is living.

Joan E Blissett

HER FACE IN AUTUMN

Those summer days play like an old movie,
Out of time moments waiting for the director's cut.
Golden fields kissed by the gentle breeze
Surrounded by enchanted green,
Trees born from a century past.
Her face in autumn caught in a picture,
So perfect her youth.
That day was cold like the ice cube
I dropped into her lemonade,
On that fire-consuming, summer's day.
Her face in autumn will never leave me,
Not until my winter song pauses my life
And we sit together again,
Beneath an eternal summer sky.

Paul Willis

LOVE TAKES WING

Love has no fear when you are near
It is the now, it is the here.
You are my day, you are my night,
You are my star, that burneth bright.

You give your love, as a rose its scent,
It lingers on with sweet content.
Lost am I in your fond embrace
Your lips, your eyes, your lovely face.

No one else could there ever be
For everything, are you, to me.
As we meet our hearts entwine
Love takes wings in flight divine.

Marian Lacy

A Mother's Love

Make up to break up in fields of long grass
Next to rivers and waterways in hazy days of sunshine.
Listen to your music or watch a film for pleasure!
Dance at a picnic! Take your clothes off in a field full of buttercups!
But watch out for the mire as you pause to admire
The beauty of a friend or a lover, and most certainly
Be careful not to be caught unawares, or
You'll certainly find yourself heading for cover!

Colette Breeze

SUMMER OF LOVE

Summer is here once again
Gardens come alive
Birds are busy mating and nesting.
Insects and flowers in full bloom
A garden to me is so special,
As my husband and myself
Used to garden together
Even when he was so poorly
He loved to be outside
The heartache I feel I can't describe
Since he passed away
I try to keep gardens nice
To keep his memory alive
So summer is so special to me
As we spent 40 years together.

N Callear

SUMMER OF 1978

In the summer of 1978
Me and Virginia made magic great
In the woods round Farney Close School
At age 13 we were no teenage fools

And in the summer of 1979
Me and Virginia made magic so fine
Till a new headmaster came around
And made the woods and ground out of bounds

But those two summers were just heaven
I was only two in 1967
The original 'summer of love'
But this was made up far from Heaven above

Back in the days of Callaghan and Thatcher
Me and Virginia and a friendly Johnny
What a shame this new headmaster
Came and destroyed our love and fun, see.

H G Griffiths

THE FRENCH POETESS

Ate breakfast at Marseilles,
Been celebration all night,
Claudette's pregnant again,
That makes eight now,
So I have to work today,
How can I in this heat,
Look, a new face,
How intriguing,
Dressed so chic,
He must have a good job,
He looks lost,
I'll help . . .
His hair is light, bleached blond,
And his eyes, blue, what secrets lie beyond,
His skin dark, the Mediterranean look,
Hid body so lean and firm to touch,
Look hard at his face I can read his every thought,
Just like a fish in the sea he knows I'm caught,
The bed a four-poster stands so tall and proud,
In beautiful Victorian lace it is endowed,
He removes my blouse the buttons carefully undone,
Over my bare shoulder his hands gently run,
He kissed my neck and then down my spine,
Slowly loosens my jean, this man is mine . . .
I open my eyes, I'm panting in the afternoon heat,
I'm in my own bed on a cool damp sheet,
Was this a fantasy or was this for real?
Is this how a French poetess should feel?

Pam Cook

TO LOUISE

From sky to new sky I have sought a reply
As to doubts, as to faith, as to end:
I have heard and I've read words both living and dead,
And knew, or so liked to pretend.
I'll be toothless and bald, a back-number so called,
But am driven to try and to try
To make some kind of mark, maybe light, maybe dark,
In the spirit of never-say-die.

Why was I put here, a sad course to steer?
Too long have I languished alone:
The past and the present, so mostly unpleasant;
The future is dark and unknown.
Come, give me a smile, to shorten the mile,
My dreams would then mostly come true,
All hope to restore, I would ask nothing more,
If I had a girl like you.

A J Vogel

OCTOBER WISDOM

Stars gaze upon the frosted air;
Somewhere a leaf shakes down a sigh.
Here in the crisp October night
We stand and watch the world go by.

No need to sail the seven seas,
No need to climb the Pyrenees.
Here in our two October hearts
Is all heartache and all heartsease.

Pamela Constantine

TRUE ROMANCE

Romantic memories of warm summer nights,
Tender kisses - sheer delights.
Loving embraces neath starlit skies,
Moonglow enhancing lovelight in your eyes.
We loved and laughed 'til the early hours,
Surrounded by the aroma of sleeping flowers.
The rising sun greets a fresh new dawning,
Azure skies herald a bright new morning.
With gentle breezes softly blowing,
The flowers are bright as if glowing.
A new day promising happiness and delight,
To prepare us for a wondrous, romantic night.

Reg Summerfield

LOVE IS

Love is all around us if we'll only stop and see,
The beauty of a blade of grass,
The leaves upon a tree.

Love is in the air with the singing of the birds,
The chortle of a baby,
The sweetest sounds you've ever heard.

Love is the sound of the rains that gently fall,
Streams that sparkle just like gems,
Trees so strong, so tall.

Love is a rainbow that arcs across the sky,
A ladybird showing off its spots,
The charm of a butterfly.

Love is the summer sun that shines from morn till night,
Love is all these wondrous things and more,
That make us feel just right.
And the flowers in the gardens
That seem to strike a pose.
But if there's one thing that portrays love
'Tis the beauty of the rose.
Love is.

Barbara Ellison

Why

Why do I love you?
No words can explain.
But, love you I do
so I'll tell you again.

I love you for the thoughtful way
you take my hand to cross the street.
The way your eyes start to shine
every time that we meet.

The way you say goodnight
with a very special kiss.
The hug that holds me tight
that I would so much miss.

So my dearest, dearest love,
these words are just for you.
Without your thoughtful loving ways
whatever would I do?

Julie Brown

DAVID AND BATHSHEBA

Over bedsprings, defamed armchairs and paraffin heaters
pan more slowly up the scarp of refuse -
emerald blinds of Ozymandias, cut low in the sale,
plots of bath tubs sprouting bulbous taps,
whatever scales to mind (it is all here),
towards a dome of diamond-blue,
wreckage of a Morris Minor.

Here David sits, lord of his domain.
Incendiary brows raise his woollen cap,
the forehead pitted with notes on a stave.
His nose anchors choppy creases.
Mistrust comes off his eyes
as ash from his fag.

His look deflects a disused railway
cropped by nettles.
A magnolia hosts her Jewish candles.

Again he turns to her he loves
and watches the woman wash,
her flesh reveal a perfect rhyme
white as two swans
skimming a restful lake, adrift.

D Hendtlass

THE HEIGHTS

How we surprise the poplars with our naked feet.
How the valley blushes under fertile glances.
How the billows rise below your muslin tallith
whispering among the billberries. How we groan
among the plane trees' razzle-dazzle sighs.
How like the raised surrender of the fig tree
you come to me, in striae of the willow-shade,
teasing Muscat from the stiffened vine.
Calm then as the walnut in deep secret halves,
caressed by citrus breeze, restraining wild garlic
on our lips, drinking-in with hot pores
the oil of pale olives, we hold hands.

Philip Burton

A LOVE POEM

If we should meet in another life,
Will you know me, love me, be my wife?
Life is so precious, each moment divine,
Comforting to think you could still be mine.

Who's to say that in centuries past,
We made a love pact that will always last?
The years roll by, like the restless sea,
We are one, that will always be.

The past, the present, the future unfolds,
Our love story may never be told.
But I'll know, love you, keep you in my heart,
With endless love, no one could tear apart.

Keith Johns

I JUST WANTED YOU

I fell for you like you fell for me
Of your love there is no doubt
I loved you then as I love you now
My thoughts just rumble out
Your face is nice, your face is kind
As I looked into your eyes
You are number one, my only one
My special kind of prize
What is this thing called chemistry?
That entwines body and soul
That lovely thing to hold so dear
That helps us reach our goal
I have walked down the road with life's heavy load
And shared my thoughts with you
Your mind met mine our thoughts sublime
'Cause I just wanted you

Rosaleen O'Brien

IMPRESSION

Hazy sunny afternoon amongst
Bluebells in the grass.
Still pillows in the sky
Hanging like washing from
A line.
Young trees shielding lovers
From possible strangers
Passing by.
Bodies snugly entied together
Clasped in heavenly copulation.
Blowing in the breeze is
Nature's spermatohore
Coming free.
Orgasmic pleasure moans a
Tune beneath the covers of
The trees.
Birds sing in harmony
Aloft in the canopy.
Soft murmurs break the
Silence of resting bodies.
The luxury of lovers'
Language fills the air:
Stirring from the grass
Carpet that they shared.
Now walking hand in hand
Leaving behind love's
Impression on the land.

Alan Holdsworth

YOU ARE

You are my music
You are my song
You are my notes
You make me sing

You are my words
You are my verse
You are my story
You make me ring

You are my thoughts
You are my feelings
You are my looks
You make me cling

You are my love
You are my kiss
You are my hopes
You make me happiness.

Ron Marland

MIDSUMMER YEARNING

It was agony being near you.
I can't get enough sweet pain
I thrill till I shake all over
That's how I want to remain.

When you ring to annoy me, I love it.
I come alive whenever you phone.
Stress drops - I float high above it.
You're my hope and I'm not alone.

But you're married, and I'm standing last
Waiting my turn in the queue.
Don't walk out. Don't break with the past.
I can't cancel it. Nor can you.

Yet you're still my living fantasy.
Though we must be apart, oh why
Does no one else exist for me
Even when we say goodbye?

My whole life got caught in suspense
On London Eye, right at the top,
With you and a longing intense
That our love-ride would never stop.

It's only my midsummer dream
Flushing my feverish brain,
Love's restless recurring theme
Too magic to ever explain.

Can I ever be near you -
Or just at the end of a phone?
Do you know how I'm longing to hear you?
Why can't I make you my own?

Dorothy

LOVE IS A CIRCLE

On summer afternoons of long ago days
When we were young and life was sweet enchantment,
We strolled the warm sea scented sands together
And planned to marry.

And through the endless sun-filled days that followed
We kissed and whispered words of love together,
Till golden autumn leaves were gently falling.
Then we were married.

You've brought me joy and love in fullest measure.
Sweet tenderness in sickness and in health
And years have passed like days of fleeting sunshine
Since we were married.

And still our love is true, our hearts are tender.
Our dreams of future days are still as bright.
You bring me warmth and hours of sweet contentment
I'm glad we married.

Anne de Menezes

STATUE OF LOVE

It was many years ago
I was hit by a thunderbolt
A million to one chance
That created a romance
She touched the corners of my mind
Raised the shutters and the blinds
From a cold dark place
That I could never escape

I took an early morning run
Along the beach
I remember the sunrise
The day was a peach
When I saw a desperate struggle
Of someone in trouble
I didn't think twice
As I battled with the tide
For an eternity
As we scrambled to the beach
Her eyes fluttered open
And I was shook and woken
From a sleep

Now I thank the sea
And the roaring tide
For all the beauty
That surrounds my life
Cos our love will always show
Sculpted in the smoothness
Of stone
Sculpted in the smoothness
Of stone . . .

Frank Howarth-Hynes

THE WEDDING ANNIVERSARY

Nine and forty years ago
seems but a moment in time,
when we made our binding vows,
which seemed to us sublime.

Time has wrought its changes
in body, soul and mind,
and sorrow has pierced our hearts,
leaving scars of a mysterious kind.

Yet joy has not deserted,
in spite of trials and sorrows,
so here's to another year,
with perhaps a few more tomorrows.

Eric Allday

A SONG TO REMIND ME

All that's left is a favourite song
Softly, now the grief has gone,
Over and over inside my head
Whether awake or in my bed.
I hear it softly and it makes me smile,
I stop and remember for just a while.
How you spoke, or moved, or stood,
And how you helped me when you could.
Always there when I needed you
Dependable, strong, always true.
Ready with a hug to comfort me,
Kind words, or just a cup of tea.
Then reality comes and I know you've gone,
And I hear again that favourite song.
A reminder of a happier time
When I was yours, and you were mine.

Haidee Williams

VISIBLY AFFECTED

I used to be fond of a rum lass,
Swarthy, eyes like almond sloes:
She sailed off with my map and compass:
Pure Romany, she comes and goes!

My new girl was a fiery redhead,
Big, clear eyes, ice-cool, light grey:
I loved her 'til my poor heart bled,
But she just seemed to melt away.

A sunny, ash-blonde, trainee vet
Took a shine to my posh Jaguar;
It matched her eyes - deep violet -
But she drove me too fast, too far.

My next love came from Derry,
Sparkling eyes of emerald green:
She loved a glass of sherry
And once had been a beauty queen!

The warmth of glowing charcoal
Reflects in Amber's eyes:
Her radiant charm my heart stole,
Sweet memories to prize.

Twins - sultry, brown-eyed brunettes -
From the sunny, Spanish main,
Amazed me with their castanets
Then dumped me in the rain.

My latest sweetheart's bashful,
Fair-haired, with eyes so blue;
I promise to be faithful,
As long as she is true.

Gareth Wynne Richards

LOVE IS

Love isn't beauty nor has any age
   or is it measured, there's nothing to gauge.
Love is a feeling that words can't describe
   love is invisible, just something inside.

Love is a strong chemical emotion
   or a churning that can cause commotion.
Love is a feeling very deep within
   or it can be risky and cause one to sin.

Love can make you happy or simply just sad
   or can make you tearful or simply just glad.
Love can give you many sleepless, restless nights
   or can cause bitter, life lasting fights.

Love can make you do some silly old things
   or can make you miserable or can make you sing.
Love is something in you, you can't describe
   or it makes you agonise and all taut inside.

Love makes you hate or feel remorse
   or it makes you dizzy and sinistrose.
Love can be in you resting peaceful and deep
   or is like a warning that goes bleep, bleep, bleep.

Love can make you great or be a stinker
   or can have you caught, hook, line and sinker.
Love is a present God gave to us all
   or is something to guide us, like a liner's landfall.

Leslie Holgate

EACH DAY

Each day I live in a brand new start
New expectations in my heart
It's more than just the way I feel
This love I have, I know it's real

Each day that comes around
I know it's life that I have found
When I go to sleep at night
Darkness is overcome by your shining light

Each day I need you more and more
How did I ever live before?
All I am is because of you
My hope and light in all I do

Each day I live is your day
Guiding me in all I say
The meaning of my life is you
Your love for me is pure and true

Amanda Steel

SUMMER ROADSIDE ROSE

I whisper to the roses, that grow by the roadside
The roadside that you walk along each day.
I tell them only, of the love I have for you.
'Yellow roses loveliest of flowers
Sweet scented roses . . .
Talk to him I pray.
Tell him that I love him
When he looks at you . . . as I know he
Will, as he passes on his way.'

I whisper to the roses, that grow by the roadside
The roadside that you walk along each day.
When the sun is warm upon them,
Or when the starlight gleams . . .
I tell them, dearest, of the love I have for you.
'Yellow roses, flecked with stardust,
Perfumed from Heaven,
Send your perfume winging on the softest summer breeze.

Drift into his window in the quiet night
While the nightingale is singing
Tell him that I love him . . .
When he looks from his window as I know he will,
To listen to the nightingale singing from the
Yellow roadside rose.'

Jennifer M Trodd

WHERE DID TRUE LOVE GO?

Love ended with progress
Today it's
Sex
Loans
Mobile phones
It's a shame
Money - name of the game
Other side of love
Like doves flown away

Mary Miller

YOUNG LOVE

Something springs into my mind
It is memories of young love gone by
That first love - so young and fresh
Sweet memories have never really left
Remember always the feelings deep
A love we were not meant to keep
The thoughts are there after all these years
We did not know it would end in tears
Fate showed the way
You were not meant to stay
I am glad to have known you is all I can say.

Linda Ann Marriott

BABY BROTHER

I remember when you arrived in the summer of July,
I recall it was the summer of July as we all complained about the heat,
Happiness, laughter and champagne filled the living room.

Everyone wanted to have a glance at you,
'Can I hold him?' they all constantly asked,
'So cute,' many said.

I pushed through the crowd with all my mighty power,
I asked if I might hold you, as I was your big sister,
Big sisters have some rights too,
Everyone nodded in agreement.

Seeing you sleep is when you are so sweet,
Other words come to mind like adorable, charming
And loved by me.

Now you are big and taller than me,
It seems I am your younger sister,
You respect and confide in me,
And I still value you.

Brother dear you now have to make tough decisions,
I hope to God you come out with flying colours
And success meets your feet.

Remember one thing I shall be on your side and stick up for you,
As I am your elder sister!

And you,
Well you still are my baby brother even when you will be 102 years old.
No matter how much taller or fatter you get!
You are my baby brother.

Parveen Kaur Saini

THE DARK OCEAN

My soul in the sea
as I wait for you my love,
my heart in the fire
as I am lost, for a while.
My mind asleep
devoured by mist,
as I am kissed, my lips
drenched in desire.
Hungry for your love
I wait for you, silence,
alone, along the beach
I fight to reach your shores.
I am far from your lips
where I want to be,
I want to be warmed
in your arms, in your love.
My soul weeps, drowns
in the dark ocean,
but I know the tide
will bring you to me, soon.

Craig Shuttleworth

ROMANTIC THOUGHTS AT EVENTIDE

'Come watch the sun my darling, as she softly sinks from view,
Combining the sea of crimson with a sky of rosy hue,
The wonder of this vista I want us both to share
Forever special to me now that I know you care.
And as we watch, the moon appears, high in the evening sky,
Then blushing hue turns navy blue, as we in love pass by.

We hear the murmuring waters of the liquid silver sea
Caressing the shores of moonlit sand, as you're caressing me.
My love is like the ocean blue, my surface cool and calm.
Tho, my undercurrents, will never do you harm.
Let's rest upon the sand dunes and observe the dawn's new light,
And as we kiss with passion, nearby gulls take flight.

The morning tide's now on the turn. The breeze blows fresh and free
As we walk upon the virgin shore, vacated by the sea.
Our magic night of passion, now a precious memory,
Forever entwined within our hearts with total empathy.
Perhaps in time we may return, I pray it will be soon,
Then, with you dear wife beside me, we'll re-live our honeymoon!'

Hazel Vambria Walters

THOUGHTS ABOUT LOVE IN OUR 50TH YEAR OF MARRIAGE

It is a good thing to be wed
And find the one who shares your bed
Remains the same from year to year
Providing love and food and cheer.
So never let your love grow cold
Not even when you have grown old
Because, within that ageing frame,
The real you still remains the same.

Ian Purvis

MISS RIGHT? ONE'S TROTH TO PLIGHT? MAYBE!

June know, that girl is really gorgeous, wonder if I have a chance?
'*July?*' asked my pal. 'No, she is truly *August*,' my mind was in a state of trance.
To the club of partnerships, please approve an application to join fortunate members,
Let the fire of love burn bright in passionate glow, rather than having to *accept embers*.
Faint heart never won fair Lady, only courtship, devotion, would culminate in a ring
My beloved was Queen of her realm, subject to her wishes, I aspired to be King.
Though hopelessly besotted, worship and admiration were conducted from afar,
Visions of close encounters, romantic smooches with my special, shining star.
Cupid's arrows pierced me deeply, though initial resistance was resolute, strong,
Now enraptured, fantasy engulfed me, my 'focus of desire' could do no wrong.
From being a carefree bachelor, my senses were hooked, bowed at her behest,
Virgos are supposed to be analytical, but palpitation erupted beneath this cotton vest.
However, there is a gulf between theory and practice, fate designed me a dreamer,
Albeit with sincere, genuine motives, not a devious or crafty schemer.
Granted poetic invitation from the publisher, I crave to write of glittering success,
Wedded bliss, ecstatic kiss, harmony to behold, joys untold, sublime caress.
Cosy cuddles, contented chats, warm embraces, fulfilled, sated sensation,
Giving and sharing, perfect pairing, protecting, caring, forming the equation.

Back to reality, my status is single, but have no gripes, grievances or moans,
Summer meant to be united, others unrequited, result of free will, not processed clones.
My angel of delight married her chosen one, but we remain firm friends,
Our bond survives passage of time, withstands all that providence sends.
Fortune may still provide a soulmate to enrich my life with circumstances conducive,
Prosperous, enjoyable, rewarding, most welcome, not in any way intrusive.
As years roll by, intrinsic feeling will never be erased, whether fanciful or real,
Only heaven can bless pure communion of spirit, which no earthly power can repeal.

Dennis Overton

MY CAT SANDY

With soft, silken fur,
Ginger and white,
The colours a-blur,
They stand out, so bright.

He likes to chase,
Bees and butterflies,
He has a beautiful face,
And big green eyes.

When he wants to play,
He will sit there and stare,
No matter what you say,
He's always there.

Helen E Schofield

HERE AND THERE

Here and there
Emotions rising
Falling as the night
The early morn
With anxious worry
Where my heart takes flight
Delicate my feelings wander
Allaying all my fears
Whilst here and there
My hopes are shattered
Soon will disappear
Silent as the sun ascending
See at last the light
My love as ever overwhelming
Peace is mine tonight
Take my hand
For I will lead you
To the brighter days
We dream the dreams
We made together
This my love I pray.

Jeanette Gaffney

BEACH GIRL

Beach girl, beach pearl -
I'll dive for you.

I'll weld into your swimmer's form.

Take off your wrap, reveal your tan
Close in the spectrum to the orange sand.
White costume iridescent -
Moon in sunlight.

I'll peel for you -
You find my body good; you make it great.
Flash back tingling on my hips
Our currents charged in sight.

Come take the plunge with me;
Let's match our thrusting limbs and muscles;
Let's arch and stretch in our exuberance;
Let's dive into a clinch.

We'll sunbathe, see our second element
Rise into vapour.

In premonition of a tidal wave
We'll peel our costumes down,
Reveal raw beauty, fuse into each other.

Your half-man muscles matching my deep thrust
Turned feminine delicate at your edges,
By your edges.

And time waits, breathless as we come;
In love we are the ocean,
All currents, eddies, tides and whirlpools,
Gales absorbed; we are the real fire water!

David Russell

OH MY LOVE

Oh my love,
You hold me,
Nothing changes,
Emotion flows and a memory is born
A timeless void forms,
Eternal love consumes,
Its loving arms surround us,
Closing our eyes forcing darkness,
Yet the mind fills with soft light,
Sensual, pure, true,
No shadows fall,
Heads pressed together we sigh,
Breathing spirits into one body,
Our soft warm lips kiss the secret
And the soul transcends into soft warm flesh,
Oh my love,
Take my hand and walk with me forever.

W T Stringfellow

SOLSTICE IN THE GLADE

The shadows deepen in sympathy
With the shade,
While sunbeams dance and play upon
The gravel floor.
As summer breezes stir the trees,
Like a rolling, ebbing tide,
Drawing its breath across a stormy shore.

Overhead the Solstice sun, radiates
Its heavenly rite.
This pierces every tree and shrub,
Within the woodland glade.
While in among the summer leaves the
Hover flies dart and play.
Then. In a flash they're gone, leaving
Only the dappled shade.

All too soon, the vision is gone, and
Reality enters my head,
As a vestige of thoughts filling
My skull.
Like a dream, I awake unto a sense
Of perfect peace,
Then return to life, refreshed within.

Andrew Whitfield

LOVE WHERE HAVE YOU GONE?

Love, love where have you gone?
Why is the world doing so much wrong?
Where is the melodious music so sweet?
Love songs that made your heart miss a beat.
Where are the couples, whispering, 'I love you'
With a beautiful wedding day in view?
Where are the churches filled to the door,
With people singing God's praises for evermore?
Where are the happy families around the fire,
And laughter filling every heart's desire?
Where is the glorious sun up on high,
The moon and the stars that light the night sky?
It seems that darkness has taken their place,
Where it once was a happy, delightful place.
God's world is now filled with misery,
Oh when will He come to set us free?
God, when will your love return to us once more?
When all know that it's You we should adore!
Joy will only come back when we all unite,
And radiate your world with glorious light.

Nicky Young

REBOUND

The thought of losing you
makes my waking hours seem like a nightmare.
You have helped me mend a shattered heart,
and yet, I am almost afraid to let you hold it
lest my nightmares become reality.

Pauline Smith

MY HYSTERECTOMY

I was poorly, didn't know why
Saw a tear in missus' eye
Couldn't eat or walk, I'd try
Drink and drink and then I'd lie

Out to the vet and there I was
Silent tears, dramatic pause
'We'll operate, curing cause'
Pinprick felt then cotton wool paws

From the dark depths to morning light
Alone and weak, gone the night
Familiar voice, welcome sight
My own missus holds me tight

Now at home I know the way
Welcome each new joyous day
Eat and walk, even run and play
Chasing birds out in the bay

Mary Hudson

ONE MAN

Who waits for me across the dark
And who there calls my name?
Imagination's lively spark
Or true love's burning flame?

Who beckons to me in the night
Where falsehoods come to play?
Romantic dreams and sweet delight
That very seldom stay?

Who tugs upon my loneliness
And tries to rock my world?
Illusion's god of love, no less
With tale and lashes curled?

Who wraps their arms about me
Whispers all I long to hear?
In shadows where I cannot see
The one man that I fear?

Kim Montia

UNREQUITED

Forever shall your memory be
Locked safe inside my heart,
Deeper than the deepest oceans,
My heart's uncharted depths.

My love for you,
The waxing moon
Can only grow till full
In darkened night, in my heart's plight
Your heart's light be my guide

I would battle my mind's daemons,
Endure the world's most cherished fear
Just for me to be with you
The love I hold most dear

My unchanging, my unfading
My love for you holds true
My forever, my eternal
Locked deep within my soul

To you I give, my untainted, my unguarded heart
To you,
My eternal love.

Gemma Guymer

SUMMER OF LOVE?

Summer. Love ran in the streets, laughing, mad.
We looked out, windows open to the crowd.
Lack of communication sat between
Us, heavy, before falling to the road
Redundant, like a sack of summer coal.
Love did not rush in, off the streets, to fill
The void. We sat, talking much, saying less.
The big, important things within your life
All seemed to happen when I was not there.

The last we had lunch, you said things won't change.
But silence fell, heavier far than lack
Of communication. We made no eye
Contact, except your glare of defiance.
What did I do? I finally broke the rule,
Unwritten, that we would never reveal
The full extent of how we felt about
Each other; once the truth was out, there would
Be no going back, and this freaked you out.

You returned to the cool and calm of work.
I also came back when my hour was up.
By then, you had told all your closest friends,
And others who were not that close at all.
The scent of ridicule hung in the air.
How strange that simple truth could be twisted
In just a quarter of an hour, at most.
Summer of love it was, but not for all.

Paul A Reeves

RESOLUTION

At first, the dim uncertainty of eyes
Took hold of me, and worked my passion to
Inferno of decision, till their blue
Transparence took the moment by surprise;
And how my wide-eyed innocence grew wise
In that platonic intercourse with you,
As if some rapture nothing could subdue
Beguiled my heart with rhapsodising sighs;
And in that instant, firm against your thighs,
I knew my soul had found her holy grail.
That morning, having heard her plaintive cries,
I dare not dream my quest could never fail.
Now, blessed with placid seas and sunlit skies,
Love bids me raise her anchor, and make sail.

S H Smith

MY FIRST LOVE - 1943

She was a little darling
her parents too were nice
but, they couldn't speak the language
received the cold shoulder
from many people in the street

Little boy
infatuated with little Esther
didn't understand one word she said
other boys in the street shouted
'Jew lover!'
she was not a Jew
she was little Esther
wish her father wouldn't wear
that funny piece of cloth on his head

One grey morning an army truck
a German soldier
driving
a Dutch policeman
her mother had difficulty
climbing in the truck
the policeman pushed her in
boy looking through the window felt sad
didn't understand
but later on in life
still remembers his first love.

J H Van Grinsven

DON'T YOU FIND IT STRANGE?

Just by chance I met you, don't you find it strange?
That we should meet so casually, you'd think it was arranged,
I didn't even know you; I'd seen you once or twice,
You'd pass me by, I'd sneak a look, I thought, she's rather nice.
I wanted to approach you, ask you for a date,
But I was sure you'd laugh at me and say, 'You're joking mate'.
Then there we were, stood side by side, waiting in a queue,
I felt your eyes upon me, so turned and smiled at you,
We chatted, oh so easily, like friends of many years,
We had so much in common, our hopes, our dreams, our fears.
I said, 'Can I see you again, take you to a dance?'
I didn't know if you'd accept, but thought I'd take the chance,
You said you'd like it very much; in fact you sounded keen,
I thought, this can't be happening, I'm sure it is a dream.
We met again, we danced all night, I fell in love with you,
I felt my heart would burst with joy, you said you loved me too.
The years passed by, we married, a family we share,
Together till eternity, so much to love and care.
There's nothing I would alter, nothing want to change,
But when you think, we met by chance, don't you find it strange?

Jim Sargant

TO MY DEAREST LOVE
(To PW)

The warmth of your sweet body,
The radiance of your soul,
Your smile, your lips, your soft blonde hair -
I want you as a whole!

May God's grace shine upon us,
And angels from above
Please guide our steps throughout the day
And sanctify our love.

Oh, how I miss your warm embrace
When fate keeps us apart,
But nought disturbs my core of peace -
Your image in my heart!

Anthony Manville

I LOVE YOU, DAVID

I'll always love you David ever so much,
As you have that special magic touch.
I'll always love you with all my heart
Join us together and let us never part.

I love you for your wisdom and your charm,
Surely you could never do me any harm.
Your love for me I'll always remember,
I think this as I love you tender.

My heart beats fast as I sing this song,
I'll think of you even when I'm in Hong Kong.
I'll give you all I have got to give,
For without you I cannot live.

I'll always love you with all my heart,
I'll also love you till death do us part.
I'll be yours forever David,
That's if you'll have me, that is.

I keep on thinking of you again and again,
Surely since knowing you life can never be the same,
I will try to be as warm and loving as I can,
Simply because I know that you are my special man.

Margaret A Greenhalgh

SUMMER DANCE

Your first expression caught my eye;
your smiling face and dark brown hair
made my heart skip a beat as I
drew near to you. A moment rare
and fleeting brought us much to share.
Unspoken feelings touched us, true
as though we'd met before. We too
seemed destined to find real romance,
electric, tangible and new,
within this moving summer dance.

Katrina Shepherd

WILDLIFE ARMAGEDDON

We cultivate the fields
and spread pesticides
on the land,
and now all the hedgerows
muted from feathered toil
stand . . .

Devoid of feathered toil
the hedgerows' stillness
blares out,
a deafening crescendo of
silence that the tears
of inactivity shout -

All nature's birds and insects
from large to very small,
the pesticides sprayed on the
fields and hedgerows is
doing for them all . . .

Peter Morriss

THE WOMAN AT THE WELL

The woman went to the well to get water
Jesus was resting, because of tired feet
Little did she know that day
That the Saviour she would meet

When she went to draw water from Jacob's well
Jesus said, 'Will you give me a drink?'
Jews don't mix with Samaritans
So what was she to think?

Jesus offered the gift of God
And the living water
She then asked him
'Are you greater than Jacob our father?'

So Jesus had to explain to her
That the water he was giving
Would be the kind of water
That would lead to eternal living

She asked Jesus for this water
Jesus said, 'Go, call your husband and come back'
At this she told him the truth
A husband she did lack

She could see he was a prophet
But what she couldn't claim
Was the Jews worshipped in Jerusalem
And their fathers on the mountain

Jesus said a time is coming, when we will worship the father
In spirit and in truth
Because when we come to Jesus
The holy spirit comes too

The woman went to tell her friends
What happened at the well
They all believed in Jesus
Because of all he had to tell

So here we have a lesson
In communication
That may bring people
To true salvation

Jean Hazell

GUESSING

From a person's face
What do you define?
Their character and
Their state of mind.
From a person's eyes
What do they denote?
Dull or alive,
Ready for a joke?
From a person's stance
What does it tell you?
Whether a person is happy
Or is feeling alright or blue.
From a person's voice
And what kind of tone
You can tell if they're happy
Or simply alone.

Mary Tickle

CONNECTED

I am that tower.
A black pinnacle against the sky.
I am your reference point.

I am the flowing track
I carry you on your journey.

Pools of water reflect the last glimmers
Of light in the dark fields.
I am they, I am the soil

I am in the earth itself,
I am in all things.

Lee Walford

SUMMER DAZE

Just one English summer day is all I desire
As I sit, snug by my flickering gas fire
Oh what I would give to be out at crack of dawn
Mowing an emerald green velvet lawn . . .

Instead of sitting, bored beside my fire
I suppose I could be out in the muddy mire
Swilling off the patio or fitting greenhouse panes
Once the rain's abated and thundered down the drains . . .

But mulling all this over I can see the sense
Of waiting 'til the wind stops blowing down the fence
And putting on hold the one thing I desire
One English summer day as I sit by my gas fire!

Betty Lightfoot

SUMMER'S BIRTH

The unseen hand that tilled and toiled
in winter's barren earth
sent forth spring shoots to herald in
the news of summer's birth.

No artist could have captured all
the colours that I saw.
As I beheld the sight I gazed
in wonder and in awe.

I heard the loveliest of songs
come from my apple tree.
He sang a song I recognise
'My Father God Loves Me'.

I smelled the air, and gazed towards
a sky of deepest blue.
Words seemed inadequate, but I
just whispered 'God, thank You.'

John Christopher

THE SEA

Some of nature's beautiful creations
are lakes, rivers and streams
and cascading waterfalls
which sparkle under the sun.

But even more wonderful - and mysterious
is the shifting sea; storm
waves break thunderously under the moon.

On calm seas we sail ships, canoes, yachts
and boats;
we surf and swim and the sea
becomes our playground.

Watching the temperate waves as they lap
over rocks and gently wash shells
to the shore, brings a serenity
which has no boundary.

Sara Newby

GREEN FINGERS

'My grandpa has green fingers,
so, by Mum, I have been told.
With them, he makes his plants and flowers grow.
He can work real wonders,
although he is very old.'
So said one little man, whose name was Joe.
'Now if I had green fingers,
mine would be a garden grand,
how many things, like Grandpa I could do!
My roses would all flourish,
at the touch of my own hand
and all around would come along to view.
There'd be a row of pansies,
in their flowerbed they'd lie,
whilst dahlias and poppies would be seen.
My hollyhocks tremendous
would reach up towards the sky,
if only I could have some fingers green.'
His Grandpa overheard him,
so, put right the little chap,
'No growth can come from fingers, yours or mine,
though we can do the planting
and give water from the tap,
all nature prospers from one source divine.'
'We thank you God Almighty,'
said two people to the Lord,
rejoicing in the beauty they could see,
their fingers placed together,
young and old, with one accord,
praised God, who caused all growth in life to be.

D J Price

GOD PROVIDES - WE ENJOY

What colour is the wind?
Rain is clear and transparent,
white snow is more a 'brilliance'
hail, seems to be all of these!

A dainty petal has texture
we touch, and feel it to be silky.
A bold red blossom we can't ignore,
cupped in our hand, dense, plush velvet.

Rugged thorny bush 'may' not please
yet housing insects, birds busy building homes.
Each and every thing 'our God' has made
variations of colour, shape and usefulness.

Oceans, mountains, lakes and sky
are far beyond our comprehension
yet-something simple like a dewdrop,
hoar frost on spider's web, He also made.

Rainbow, rock formations, magnificence.
Remedial warmth, cleansing waters
are only part of our God's goodness.
His love and care in abundance, we share.

Elements, water, light and dark
heat and cold, night and day.
Seasons, the 'wonders' that they bring,
we're in the 'midst' of all that God planned.

Creation could not just be 'written' in a book
it cannot be 'explained' as such.
All our 'senses' have to take it in,
God's presence a 'bonus' as we communicate
with His creation, His 'loving nature', His world.
Nature is one way that reveals God's existence!

Beryl Lenihan

ODE TO NIGHTFALL

Dusk flows gently over the fields
Trees stand in evening prayer . . .
Cows quietly graze, birds are at roost.
No disturbance of peace is here.
A glowing sun sank away in the west
And red silken skies linger on . . .
A crescent moon rising -
A star shining bright -
The clouds having tarried are gone.
Night-time enters in grey-blue cloak.
A distant owl hoots with great zest . . .
Flowers tight close as darkness deepens . . .
    Nature at last is at rest.

Joan Lewington

MIDSUMMER FOXGLOVES

Standing tall, trailing between ivied trees,
Each foxglove awaits the magic of midsummer.
Gossamer wings flutter by shady ferns
And sunlight filters through the damp earth.
Grey stems give life to pale green leaves,
Finely striped and veined:
Cabbage coloured.
Emerging darker, deep below,
Buds like apple blossom swell
And trumpets of pink, purple or paler, faded bells
Reveal hollow tunnels:
Foxed, speckled or spotted;
To attract bees or fairies
Through the drowsy afternoon.

Penelope Freeston

CHANGES

In life there are so many changes:
From childhood to adulthood,
From school to college, from college to work,
From singleness to marriage,
From being a couple to starting a family,
The void created when the children leave home,
Moving house, changing your job,
The death of a loved one.

Some people dislike any kind of change
They would far rather stay the same,
But change is part of life . . .
Sometimes we need to move on.
A new job can be a challenge,
A family can push us to our limits -
We need to pray for patience and wisdom
In the disciplining of our children.

We must be more open to change,
To welcome change when it knocks at our door.
We can learn from all of life's experiences . . .
By the time we've reached old age
We'll have so much wisdom to share!

Cathy Mearman

After Winter

I went for a walk in the evening
   The sunset, enchanting, divine,
Horizon was glowing in beauty
   This wonderful picture was mine.
The sparkling sea was like diamonds
   Its vastness and depth who could know?
For God in His wisdom created
   The elements so they could show
Their beauty in evening at twilight
   What bliss at the end of a day.
Thank God for sight to gaze at a heaven,
   Love manifest in such display.

Margaret Carter

SUMMER DAY

I sit in the garden
And all around
Is the sound
Of people, living;
Of splashing pools and barbecuing
And all the things that people are doing;
The music's beat thudding through the heat
And voices raised, all trying to compete -
People, living.

And it's all because of Jesus, two thousand years ago,
All because of Jesus -
And I wonder - do they know?

Joy Jenkins

First Light

Dawn slowly rising,
From the siesta,
Night obscured,

From the dark cell,
Where in frozen motion,
The predator held you,

Pale orb,
Silently stealing,
From your horizon rendezvous,

Where the barriers of time,
Restricted your motion,
Until the given hour,

Higher you rise,
Abandoning the host,
Soon all will awake,

Your spirit set free,
High into sapphire skies,
Where you will shine down.

Ann G Wallace

INSIDE, LOOKING OUT

As I stand at the sink washing dishes
And look out on the world every day,
I wonder at each new marvel
A loving God sends our way.

Seasons come and seasons go,
Kitchen view plays continuous scenes
To lift my spirits, boost my faith
And show me where God has been.

Just now He's in skeletal branches
Filling them with sap anew,
Plumping buds to burst wide open,
Treading softly on crystal dew.

He's raised green sheaths of daffodils
During long, dark, winter morns,
Bulbous, lemon tips remind me soon
Spring will blow their golden horns.

He's enticed downy-feathered fledglings
From the shelter of fragile eggs
To find the scraps on my bird-tray,
Such delicate beauty on spindly legs!

He's swept the dark clouds of winter
To give a bluer, cloud-tipped sky,
Tree branches stretch to touch them,
A soft green tinge on them I spy.

As spring days lengthen into summer,
I'll watch new panoramas unfold,
See His glories open into fulfilment,
The contrasts, exciting and bold.

Pat Heppel

BASIC ORIENTATION

The main build-up of green lichen on the trunk of a tree
will be on its west side, if well exposed, you look and see.

Position this lichen to your left and stand still.
You are now facing south, because it's your will.

When at sea there are no trees to give a clue
but the sun will rise every morning on cue.

The early morning sunrise shining bright
indicates east and should be placed to your right.

North is straight ahead and no longer a mystery
because your right side is facing easterly.

If not too cloudy the sun is seen sinking in the west
with a little effort it's easy to work out the rest.

So if ever you are lost and in some despair
remember these guide lines and be aware.

Don't forget the small pocket compass,
this indicates north without impasse.

Brian Bates

APOCALYPSE

The people hurry, scurry, why do they worry?
Greed and wealth and all things material is what they worship.
This is the altar, this is their creed,
They do not listen, they do not heed.
Planet Earth is mother to us all,
She created us and she will make us fall,
We take, we do not give,
By doing this we will lose the right to live.
We poison the Earth, we sour the water,
All will be gone in the last quarter.
The air we breathe is tainted,
By breathing it we will be like lambs going for slaughter.
Planet Earth is a beautiful place
But because of us there will be no space.
Nature, the supreme force, God, call it what you will.
It is the one we finally will have to reckon with.
It waits, the time is nigh when terror will fall from the skies.
There will be nowhere to hide, nothing to keep.
A ball of fire and lightning across this Earth will race,
Destroying all and everything who stand in its face.
The seas will boil, the rivers run dry,
Everything but everything will completely die.
The planet will turn cold and ice will begin to creep,
The air will be still, and then the final sleep.
The Earth will be dead, a ghastly place
And confined to the universe to spin in space.
It is finished, man is dead, gone forever in a twinkling
If, but if, he only had had an inkling.

Carl Kemper

GULF COAST SUNSET

We walked the beach at sunset along the Gulf coast shore
The ebb tide slowly lapping at twilight's opening door

The heat of day subsided, the light a burnished peach
We searched around for seashells and collected half the beach

Pelicans flew off homewards to the harbour's wooden piles
Fishing in the wave-tops to sustain their homeward miles

Across the sea, the sunlight, carved a fluid road of gold
The sun described its final arc as it slipped from daytime's hold

The fading sun glowed redly, its last rays spreading free
First a bright red ball of fire, then an eyebrow on the sea

The pink-edged clouds grew darker as the sun sank further west
And in the closing of a summer day the birds flew to their rest

The horizon slowly faded to a common twilight hue
And in this light we walked the beach as lovers often do

To walk the beach at sunset along the Gulf coast shore
Is to touch a bit of paradise

Who could ask for more?

Ray Ryan

THE BIG FLOOD

The country has been flooded
Destruction everywhere
The rivers all have burst their banks
There is water where there once were towns
People have worked so hard
To secure their homes
Now they have lost possessions
Everything they owned
Oh Lord look down on these people
And take the floods away
Help them build a new life
In you I have such faith

G Morrisey

LIFE OF THE SEEDS

Through country lanes, past country fields
From light green grass to rugged browns,
Short or long grass, from ruggedly ploughed brown fields,
How strange the land looks with care and love the seeds grow,
From the spring's breeze, and care of all that's
Growing to the cutting at the end of the season.

With the grace of the breezes in the summer's sun
So great and pleasant are the gardens across the land,
From the green fields, to the brightness of the mixed coloured flowers,

Spotted across the land are barns,
Farmhouses, in the fresh green fields, herd of cows roam the field,
With sheep in adjoining field slowly grazing,
How great the land is, so fresh and clean,
From one so great he created the seas,
He created the land so fresh and great,
As the sun shines all the seeds have developed
So fresh and brightly coloured.

From season to season the land changes
From the cold wintry days to the fresh warm summer's days,
How wonderful the Earth takes each different season,
From baron land to a land so fresh and green
Through to lighter yellow plants spread in the fields
So freshly swaying in the warm summer's breeze.

Sharon Joy Wandless

STOP

Who will eat the fish
With mercury
On their dish?
Not to mention the trout,
Fed on hormones too,
Who will want to eat
Medicine made out of
Tigers' bones?
The elephants and their horns,
By the humans purposely worn.

Be warned, humans,
We are next,
Exploited like the animals,
It can well be your turn next.
Wake up.
It's the harm we are doing them,
It's the harm we are doing to ourselves.
It's not too late,
Put the wrong,
Right.

A Bhambra

THROUGH THE WINDOW AT MY WORLD

I stare out through a window, at a still and dim-lit sky,
I wonder, are you out there, and I always wonder why
I didn't have the courage, I guess I didn't care,
To say how much I loved you, whilst you were standing there,
I know deep down my feelings bring me sorrow and some pain,
It hurts each night, whilst I wait for you to come back again,
You thought you didn't matter, it was me who made you go,
I learnt a valuable lesson that I did love you so,
And as your footsteps faded, you walked into the past,
Now I have no will to live, no other love will last,
If you're listening out there will you please believe I care,
If I look through my window tonight, let your face be there.

Janet Kelly

CONCRETE HOME

I saw a man living on the street today
Sad, lonely and mad in some way
I spoke to him for an hour or two
Then left him alone to observe the view.

I passed a woman just yesterday
Drunk and confused in a strange sort of way
She told me she lived in a squat that was dark
I told her I lived in a house by the park.

I met some friends at a quarter to three
They were happy and content as most should be
Their wives they said were becoming a bind
I just nodded and thought of outside.

I observed a man just tonight
A bottle in his hand, eyes full of fright
He told me he had no place to go
I gave him some cash and replied, 'I know.'

Steve Pape

NEVER TOO OLD TO LEARN

The most unlikely footballer ever turned out for our team yesterday,
With shirt much too large and cuffs dangly, no one knew quite
what on earth to say.
He'll never kick the ball with those boots on, they should have
gone out with the ark,
What on earth is the manager thinking? We'll be the laughing stock
of the whole park!

The referee blows his whistle to kick off and right away the
other team runs off to score,
The lads are in for a hiding today. So what's new, we've been here
so often before.
Heads droop as usual but that's nothing amiss, we all know
confidence is a peculiar thing,
But we are all ignorant on just what to do, so shouts of
admonishment and cajoling will ring.

Hello, what is that? What's happening there? This is a new one
and a shock to us all,
That little ragamuffin, him least likely to succeed is encouraging
and shouting for the ball.
His team mates look up to see who is vocal and from his endeavour
take great heart,
The chain reaction that this lad ignites is very infectious it gives
the whole team a kick-start.

Humbly we stand at the side of the pitch, squirming at our initial
uncharitable thoughts,
For this wee young lad with his two left feet freely introduced
a greater talent to a team out of sorts.
The will to succeed and to never give up meant he'd yield
not even an inch in his desire,
Our adult blinkers came off as our twelve year olds played
inspired by that lad full of fire.

R Grainger

BRUNCH

CO_2 is bad for you but plants just think it's great
Breakfast, lunch and supper, they slice it on their plates
Teatime's rather special though, they give themselves a break
Bees come collecting pollen so flowers can have some cake

The pollen becomes honey, I'm sure as we all know
Which makes nice cakes for ducks and drakes we go out feeding - so
By broadcasting the crumbs about we've brought there in our cars
The plants too get some cake to eat - or store it up in jars

Which through the longest winter days provide such sustenance
For tea to be a pleasant change from CO_2 much brunch

Peter Asher

BIG SHOT!

She, feeling unhappy and cross,
Decided to leave home,
Quitting country for mid-town chaos,
Or head for aerodrome.

Keeping departure to herself,
Packed her case secretly,
Returned to position on the shelf,
Waiting impatiently.

After an endless duration
Parents settled for night,
Seized her chance and left. Which direction?
Should she turn left or right?

Opted left and began long trek,
Case was hitting her legs,
Overweight; pulling on nape of neck,
Longed for a lift to beg.

Too tired to take another step,
Idea began to rue,
She plonked herself on the back doorstep,
Of someone kind she knew.

After a while the door opened,
Found with case, hat askew,
'I've left home!' she announced to good friend,
'Can I live here with you?'

Familiar chum much amused,
Asked her to smile, say cheese,
Took photo, rang her mother, bemused,
How daughter left with ease.

Knew four year old to be earnest,
The journey to next door,
Preferred to mishap with motorist,
Boded urge to explore.

Countries, knowledge and business swot
Ventures from Welwyn plot
Still peruses initial snapshot
When she aged four 'big shot'.

Hilary Jill Robson

THE ZOO

The lion let out a deafening roar,
and stamped a paw upon the floor,
the reason for this fit of rage,
the visitors were at the zebra's cage.

I'm supposed to be the jungle king,
the monarch of the circus ring,
I'm the sure-footed beast, with never a fall,
admired by many, but feared by all.

What's so special about these stripes,
I feel like playing those Scottish pipes,
to make them dance a jig with glee,
and then they'll all come back to me.

They like to see me through the bars,
I'd like to see the moon and stars,
to roam about, and feel more free,
but I guess this is where my life will be.

Still it could be worse, I don't do much,
I'm not an animal folk love to touch,
I'm like a show at which they peep,
But I'm very proud to earn my keep!

Edith Antrobus

CHRISTMAS NIGHT

The twinkling stars were shining bright
Upon the silent, waiting ground
And all the earth was bathed in light.

The shepherds watched their flocks by night
Kept safe where prowling wolves abound
The twinkling stars were shining bright.

An angel arrayed all in white
Was on a joyful mission-bound
And all the earth was bathed in light.

He told the shepherds of the mite
Newborn who would all men astound
The twinkling stars were shining bright.

Three wise men gazing, saw the sight
Of guiding star, they looked around
And all the earth was bathed in light.

The star did all the men excite
Who journeying, the baby found.
The twinkling stars were shining bright
And all the earth was bathed in light.

Joyce M Turner

TEACHINGS

There is a season
For every season
When the seasons are

There is a sky
Of many skies
Wherein one sky exists

There is a God
Of many gods
Where one god is alone

There is a book
Of many books
Wherein the answers lie.

Cathrine Campbell Rodgers

THE LESSON

How could I know that this was just a game,
You loved to play, a journey just begun.
That once you knew that you had lit the flame,
The conquest made, you looked elsewhere for fun.

For I had never been in love before,
I treasured every honeyed word you said.
Your practised kisses thrilled me to the core,
I sweetly dreamed one day we would be wed.

But when I saw that this would never be,
Such desolation seeped into my soul.
Was all romance indeed a fallacy?
Do other men act out this clever role?

Oh well, for me a lesson learned, and yet,
I have my life to live, and I am free.
So when one day, another man I've met,
Then, next time, so much wiser I shall be.

Jean Gray

No Longer a Joke

A man curled up in a ball.
His body bony,
his eyes nearly closed.
No,
he's not asleep!
He's dying of thirst and hunger,
the sun makes his thirst grow.
We see him on the tele,
covered in flies.
Disease and famine,
before our eyes.
But what I didn't realise,
until five seconds ago,
is that people ain't a TV show.
They breathe, they move,
they see, they feel,
and the world is so wrapped up
in money,
that it keeps its eyes closed!

Kevin Challis

BOOK OF LIFE

Angels ventured to earth last night,
In a beautiful beam
Of heavenly light.
In their blissful arms
They held the lambs,
Slaughtered for food in all the lands.
These angels arrived from heaven above,
To beg mankind,
For compassion and love.
To speak up for the lambs,
Millions and more,
Who endlessly trot through the heavenly door.
From stained woolly coats,
Acres of blood untold,
Stretch from earth to heaven
Till they reach the fold.
God will name all who create
This murder and strife.
Scribing all of their names
In his 'Judgement of Life'.

Patricia Spencer

MISSING YOU

Love is a fat onion
Immured in old, cold soil
With long leaves lowing,
As if it could be real -
Your presence as a going
With long leaves lowing.

Nicola Barnes

A SOFT TOUCH
(Dedicated to Mishka and Sasha)

They look at me - their eyes beguile
a mouth curves in a gentle smile -
you can't feel hungry - not again
I give a sigh that is in vain.

They lick their lips - and give a purr -
these tiny ones with coal-black fur.
'Please fill our dish.' What would you like?
'A little fish would taste all right
before we sing with purr delight -
then keep you warm throughout the night.'

With love like this it's plain to see -
they'll always have their way with me;
my two black cats whom I adore -
just know I'm putty in their paws!

Anita Richards

THE PLAN IS

'The plan is, there is no plan'
said the major to the minor
'We'll spend our time, in shallow rhymes
round the table at the diner
there'll be no aims or objectives
no long or short term goals
we conclude, that talk is rude
and vanishes in black holes
no 14 pointed strategy
no agenda, no pretence
we'll plan our coup, by saying boo!
and using common sense
no filofax or fiction
no theory close at hand
and as they look through it and wonder how we'll do it
we'll say there is no plan.'

F McFaul

A JOURNEY TO REALITY

There's a journey I must make, that will cause my heart to break,
A bereavement, always puts me to the test,
I already feel the chill of that graveyard on the hill,
Telling me I'm just as mortal as the rest.

I will see those folk again, whom I meet just now and then,
When occasions such as this one come around,
And once again I'll find, we're more apt to speak our mind,
When we gather round an opening in the ground.

Standing there distraught with grief, I will stare in disbelief,
At the coffin of the one who had to go,
I'll agree they were the best, to have known them, I'd been blest,
It's so sad they had to die! Before I'd know.

Had they dreamed of wealth and fame, or had cause for guilt or shame?
Those are things they'd have in common with us all,
There's no sin in fame or wealth, if they make a better self,
And from grace, we know the saintliest can fall.

Oh why is it that we wait till a loved one meets their fate
Then attempt to put a halo round their head?
Love and praise when they're alive might just help them to survive,
But none of those can help them when they're dead.

If there's something in your heart, that you're longing to impart,
Just a little bit of self you want to give,
Don't be selfish and conceal, the emotion that you feel,
You should show it, let folk know it, while they live.

Matthew L Burns

Happiness

Dear Jesus joy of man's destiny

We pray for happiness in our family.

We pray for your gift of joy and happiness to lighten our walk
With you -

Happiness in service
Happiness in loving relationships,
Happiness in creation,
Happiness in contentment,
Happiness in health.

Let our family feel and know, please Jesus, a touch of your humour,
in our lives; by your healing power and saving grace.

Happiness with time and joy in space.
Happiness for others and to come from others too.
Happiness especially to give to children.

With thanks for joy given to me by Jesus, Amen.

Joan Sansom

MY OFFERING

I offer You my hurt, Lord,
The things that trouble me;
My sin and my temptation,
For You alone can free.
I offer You my pain, Lord,
For You can understand.
The weakness of my body
I place into Your hand.

I offer You my darkness,
My deepest, inmost night,
That You might share it with me
And shed Your holy light.
I offer You my tiredness,
So busy is the day.
You offer strength and comfort
Along life's toilsome way.

I offer You my day, Lord,
The mundane tasks I share,
I offer You the night hours
And know You will be there.
I offer You my all, Lord -
May everything I do
Be consecrated wholly,
My blessed Lord, to You.

You took the bread of suffering,
You bore it all for me.
You take my heavy burdens,
And in You I am free.

Ann S Clifton

SHARE A PRAYER

A new home.
It feels so strange Lord.
I know you are there and always are,
Yet I feel tears in my eyes.
I know you love me Lord,
But inside I'm all mixed up.
Help me Lord to remember to trust in you,
Never to doubt,
Never to forget you.
Your love is for the taking as you wrap your arms around me.
May I take that out my new door and give as you give to me.
And I know then it will not feel so strange
I ask for that strength,
Seek for guidance and thank you for being here on this earth for me.
                                                                                 Amen

Anne Macleod

JUST OUT OF REACH

Our chosen place, dear one,
to lie beneath this beech
each just out of reach.

At perfect rest, my love;
so let the sorrows cease.
Commune content in silent peace.

No longer now the pain,
so let this rippling stream
carry forth our earthly dream.

My voice calls out to you,
and here beneath our tree
I feel you nearer me.

Until the great day dawns
when love melts into love
in unknown worlds above.

Cynthia Smith

RELAX ME LORD

Lord, there are so many lessons
I have still to learn,
But for the moment, teach me I pray
How to relax,
How to relax in you.
I need to be able to feel you Lord
Every minute of the day.
Not just when I chat with you at the beginning,
Or when we come together at the close.
I want to experience
A closeness with you every minute.
I tell myself I am relaxed and resting in you,
But then something happens,
And in a moment I am thrown in a sea,
The waters of frustration swirl round me,
And I am sinking,
I am not relaxed at all.
I fight my way back to the surface Lord,
I am aware that I have not learnt this lesson,
Not properly.
Go on teaching me Lord, until it hurts.
For I cannot learn this lesson Lord,
I cannot be your disciple.
I cannot proclaim to others,
What I have not allowed you to do for me.
So relax me Lord,
Filter your peace right into my soul.

Sandra J Walker

HOLDING MY HAND

Faceless in an invisible field
Stone deaf in a silent land
Empty of harvest yield
Yet still he holds my hand.
Voiceless in the desert of dry hope
Deep in a waterless land
Lost upon a chill slope
Yet still he holds my hand.
Now resentful in the icy rain
By cold winds fanned
I blame him for my pain
Yet still he holds my hand.

Pat Bidmead

THE WORD

Friendships have been broken
By a thoughtless word that's spoken
Tender feelings easy bruise
When angry spiteful words are used
So do not even speak in fun
The word to injure anyone
Think a little, change your mind
Then answer, but be very kind

Kathleen Dodd

DEAR GOD

Please make me healthy and wise
Make me use my brains and my eyes
Wonderful gifts, graciously given
So I put them to work, don't need to be driven

My two eyes to see all the good things in life
To close on all the trouble and strife
You gave me brains to help my fellow men
May I follow that rule steadfastly! Amen!

You gave me a heart with so much love in it
To help other people and live every minute
To work till I drop if that is needed
As long as I'm there with the help that is needed

You gave me a mouth to praise you on high
To keep to your rules and never say die
Thank you God for letting me shine
You in your heaven and I in mine

Marjorie Wagg

LOADING UP

Fill the emptiness of my heart
with ballast of your love.
Stack carefully loving thoughts
in the warehouse of my mind.
Pour forth your healing spirit
in the void that is my soul.
Lord, please do your utmost
to help to make me whole.

Frank Keetley

A DAY AT THE BEACH

The beach was crowded
Though the wind blew.
Tourists thronged
They'd see it through.

The sea smelt of fish
And the beach was on a slope.
Even the sea had receded
Leaving flotsam and bits of rope.

We were getting hungry
Our stomachs rumbling.
Someone didn't like the view
Grannies always grumbling.

The air was full of laughter
And bouncing plastic balls.
I shivered in my trunks
And wished I'd worn my thermals.

The salad's full of flies
And the tea's getting cold.
It's the last time I come here
Or so I've been told.

We're packing up
And starting to head for home.
Next time I do this
I'll be coming on my own.

Mick Rose

ANYTIME, ANYWHERE

At truly any time, and equally anywhere
I can lift my voice to the Lord in prayer,
Yes, whatever the moment, or whatever the place
I boldly can come to the throne of grace;
And whether in a crowd, or completely alone
I can, to the Father, make my every need known;
For whether with spoken word, or inaudibly,
I confidently can say 'Thou God hearest me.'

As I tread city sidewalks, with the traffic racing by
I can ask for the wisdom which comes from on high;
And alone with nature, where creation's glories blaze,
I can give voice to a heart o'erflowing with thankful praise;
When soaking in the bath, or taking a pleasant shower,
I can ask for the filling of the Holy Ghost's power;
And when behind the wheel, at the car's controls,
I can beseech the Lord to save precious souls.

Whenever I need courage to face some daunting task,
I can come to the One who invites us to 'Ask',
And when I crave the strength not found in myself,
I know God will provide, according to His boundless wealth;
And should someday painful illness lay my body low
Then, closer than a brother, His friendship I know,
Where, if too weak e'en to speak, or to lift up mine eyes,
He will attend to, hear and answer my heart's silent cries.

I may ne'er enter the palace of an earthly king,
Yet how great is my privilege, I my petitions can bring
To the royal courts of the heavenly one,
The way now made open through the blood of His Son,
And open to all, whate'er their colour, class or race,
Who approach in Christ's merits, trusting in God's grace,
Having come to the cross, and found so great salvation,
And trusting now for prayer answers beyond all expectation.

Where shall I go from his Spirit, or from His presence flee?
Neither to the heights of heaven, nor in the deepest sea:
Lord, you are ever present, wherever I may be,
And you know and you care intimately about me;
Yes, your all-seeing eyes are in every place,
That you may succour, strengthen and give abundant grace,
So, faithful Lord, I thank you for always being there,
My dearest friend I can call on - anytime, anywhere.

Ian Caughey

Memory-Kept Kisses

The anguish of waiting goes on like a rainy day,
Sighs a zillion spent on nothingness, deep, desperate discontent,
A band of stress tied around the head,
Wringing hands cracked, beaten shrunken ever-hopeful heart.

Will it be this moment or the next?
Will it be soft like rubbing a baby's head on my bottom lip?
Memory of purity stored and kept,

Will it deepen sweet like ripe soft fruit wet lips savouring indulgently?
Will it be savage as with greedy fighting dog lips like shouting,
                                            going for the kill?
Arguing, wiping away with lips, not the back of your hand.

The foul taste of deceit, hasty unbelievably cruel words salty
                                with tears peppered with apologies,

Still the waiting goes on, along with the sighs for desired kisses
                                  given with best love always.

D P R Stockton

... AND JESUS SPOKE!

'Aye, aye' quo she, 'a cup o tea
wid ging doon verra weel,
but gin the rain comes teemin' doon
a'd nae get through ma dreel.
A'll waursel on nae faur ahint
till lousin' time comes bye
then a'll hae a cup tae warm the hert
'fore ca-in in the kye.
Thur autumn days is shorter nou
an' muckle's tae be dune,
if time's aa spent in drinking tea
a'd be workin' by the mune.
A'll thank ye kindly aa the same.
A'm tired, as weel ye ken
but a'll dae ma stint in aa ma dreels
afore a'm ca'ed richt ben!'
'Nae so, ma lass! Ye're sairly bent.
Awa an' hae yeir tea! Forget the kye
an' aa the rest, an' leave it lass, tae me!'

Andrew Duncan

LIFE WASN'T ALWAYS LIKE THIS

When you're just feeling down and out
And all you want to do is scream and shout
You would like to pull yourself together
But something's holding you back like a tether
It's like you're just groping in the dark
With your only light an occasional spark
If only everything was bright and clear
Instead of the doom, gloom and fear
And the realisation that others don't understand
They give you a push when you need a hand
The strangest feeling when you just can't cope
You're down so low all you have now is hope
For you know that it wasn't always like this
For life without depression can be bliss

Meg Bremner

POETRY

The above is an art as a matter of fact,
Like words strung together with a bit of tact
The way we think, the way we may act
Like signing our name to some kind of pact

Like Rabbie and Shakespeare they had it all
But what they had made them stand tall
Amongst the rich and amongst the poor
Both names are now history, 'end of story'.

Joseph Broadley

To A Muse

I cast stones at the lilies of Giverny
Claude almost threw a fit
I illuminated the book of Kells
A mad monk helped a bit
I splashed at Alma Tadema
As I sprawled in my sunken bath
When I dropped my straps for Titian
We got drunk and had a laugh
On the chapel scaffold I did a Tarantella
Caught the eye of Buonarotti
Stepping off, I danced on air
Giggling as he couldnotti.
I dallied with Dali
Got horny with Hornel
Manet was one of many . . .
Oh, how I teased poor Raphael
Creating the backdrop
That's my artistic bent
I nodded with Picasso
Though I never knew what he meant
I drove dear Luke to madness
The artist's patron, their saint
He inspired landscapes and cherubs
Yet breasts were what they would paint
I mused, I was a muse amused, how amusing
The original centrespread
My immortal smile can bewitch you
Da Vinci knew . . . but he's dead.

Jeanette Latta

MEMORIES OF NORTHLANDS

Let me take the northern road that leads me back again,
The heather-covered hillside I look for now in vain,
I long to go where as a boy I stood in days of yore,
Where lofty peaks stand tall and proud near a highland shore.

To wander now and where once before I stood with fellow men,
I see again in my mind's eye the wild deserted glen,
The curlew's haunting, sad refrain, stirs my memory still,
Where red deer stand with heads held high beside a mountain rill.

Let me take the northern road I see now in my dreams,
And stand once more to see again the everlasting streams,
Where waters cascade to the sea and mighty salmon leap,
Towering mountains guard the glens, their secrets still to keep.

Nothing mars the silence in this vast and lonely place,
Here in rugged moorland is tranquillity and space,
It seems that time now here stands still and sheds a heavy load,
This is why I long to take once more the northern road.

A H Thomson

EVACUATION OF THE CITIES, SEPTEMBER 1939

Out of the squalor
of soot-covered slums
marched an army of children,
labelled and counted,
clutching bundles of clothing
in brown paper parcels,
gas masks slung
around grubby thin necks.

Bewildered and scared,
torn from their Mams,
herded on trains,
unwillingly taken
to live among strangers,
they discovered a land
of green grass and trees,
where milk grew in cows
and birds flew uncaged.

Left in the cities
swept clean of their future,
grieving parents wept.

Doreen Dean

The Hobble Gobble Man

The Hobble Gobble Man lives in the evergreen tree
He has no family to call his own or friends to share his tea

So he set about to devise a plan and laid it out with care
With luck he would catch a friend who could stay to tea and share

He caught a little bull frog, a vivid emerald green
He took him in his tree house and told him of his dream

The bull frog did a hop and croak and then he did agree
He would be his little friend and stay and have some tea

So now the Hobble Gobble Man is as happy as can be
For now he has a little pal who stays with him for tea

Barbara Tyers

HOAX NO JOKE

All you little kids out there,
When you dial the brigade, 999,
You could be putting someone's life,
Right there on the line.
Someone else might need them,
While they're answering your hoax,
It might be a tiny baby,
- Or maybe some old folks.
So before you dial that number,
- Before you make that call,
It may be one of your family in need,
- It might even be them all.

Joyce Clegg

THE GRIMGIN MAN

Whoever thought of the Grimgin Man?
Whoever thought he'd smite our land?
Whoever thought he'd rule our plains,
that he'd deal the final hand?

Whoever thought of him when he was alone?
Whoever thought of him out in the cold?
Whoever thought of a prayer for him,
so that he may be spared?

Whoever thought of helping him when he was shunned?
Whoever thought they should?
Whoever thought they had time to spare
so he wouldn't grow cold?

Whoever thought he was worth a dime?
Whoever thought they had the time?
Whoever thought they'd ever regret it,
leaving him to grow old?

Whoever thought he'd get his revenge?
Whoever thought he wouldn't win in the end
Whoever thought it'd be like this,
not he, who thought someone cared?

Whoever thought of the Grimgin Man?
Whoever thought he'd smite our land?
Whoever thought of the Grimgin Man,
that he'd deal the final hand?

Whoever thought of the poor Grimgin Man?

Julie Ann Evans

CARTIER CAT

Sitting upright, feline wise,
Owl-like,
Topaz for eyes.

Scanning the lane in proud pose,
Grand dame,
Jet is her nose.

Smiling, the lips a cruel sheath,
Diamond-edged
Pearls for teeth.

Licking with care the manicured paws,
Hidden, sly,
Opal the claws.

Thinking of lovers, how they'd sung,
Passion-led,
Coral her tongue.

Stretching the sinews of pliant silk,
Oiled in liquid
Gold, not milk.

Flexing her body on weathered stones,
Muscles strung
On platinum bones.

Wearing her worth with casual stare,
Living jewel
Of craftsman's care.

Jane Taylor

SO I AM BLACK

In McDonald's on Saturday night
waiting for the film, we had quite a fright.
A group of youngsters worse for beer
tormented a big black man, who had no fear.
As our party quietly slipped away
distancing ourselves from the fray,
voices were raised and violence about to erupt.
Shocked by the scene, it seemed
so mean
that a black man should have all this fuss.
All he wanted was a quiet coke
not a fight with a white drunken bloke.
'Look here Whitey,' he screamed
as in anger he leaned over to land
him a punch.
The white lad ran away, to fight again
another day
But it had soured the evening for us.

Rosemary C Whatling

PESTILENT DOORS

Nutters' Park. (we call the asylum)
Is no better in the dark,

Us werewolves in, thru green doors,
Smarties put on shaky paws,

Nasty nightmares following nightly hypnotics,

Morning poison, waking up for tea
No hope on the horizon, can I see,

Us all talking, I turn the radio on
I do hope lunch won't be long,

If all the doctors could be sent away,
All the pills thrown away

And Nutters' Park left behind
I think that that would clear my mind.

Simon Morton

1984-1999

We had a little dog, Scamp was his name,
Playing ball was his favourite game.
For my fortieth birthday he was bought,
My son knew he was a special sort.
We would walk for miles along the canal path,
When we returned, he would need a bath.
Someone at the door, he'd make sure they didn't stay.
When we were at work he'd go for a walk with Kay.
We would walk round the ponds every day,
If he met Mary with her dog, he'd love to play.
He would lie out on the lawn in the sun
And gave us hours of laughter and fun.
No more walking out in the rain,
Things will never be the same.
Now he's gone days seem long.

J Noble

Hangman's Noose

My hand touching her soft face
As I hold her in a fond embrace
Her ruby lips shine in the dusky light
Soon be farewell as it is nearing night
Will we meet again?
The years will pass in great pain
To be parted from your tender touch
My sweet dear whom I love so much.

The noose will soon be tight around my neck
Trapdoor will give way, is there hope yet?
I hear the guard's footsteps on cobbles clear
It is surely true they are coming near
I'll never see the light of another day
Please priest come so I may pray
Unburden all my woes and sorrows
For there will never be a tomorrow

The hangman's noose is around my neck
I can see my sweet love, I'll be back yet
The trapdoor opens, I'm in the air
See her face so beautiful and fair
Feel I am floating far beyond
Over valley, fields and a pond
Where my love sits full of tears
I brush her face as I go near
We will meet again my dear.

Eunice Neale

WHO WALKED BEFORE

As I learn of those who walked before
In the days of summer then winter too
Some were young yet like me some had grown old
I have no photograph of you all so I am told.

As I learn of those who walked before
How old were they all as they passed away
Nobody knows really for many things are in doubt
I have no photograph of you all so I am told.

As I learn of those who walked before
I hope I can meet you in heaven
Or maybe hell is where you all finally rest
I have no photograph of you all so I am told.

Keith L Powell

THE OLD CEMETERY

Squirrels and foxes, insects and rats,
All manner of birds, wild flowers and bats,
Walkers and joggers running their course,
The occasional policeman astride a horse.

Perverts and muggers with stolen loot,
A discarded condom, an old worn out boot,
Rubbish and junk all over the place,
This just won't do, it's such a disgrace.

Tombstones and graves all broken and trashed,
Crosses and statues vandalised and smashed,
Family vaults that are showing neglect,
Fallen memorials that once were erect.

Rusty old railing and broken benches,
Great big potholes and dug out trenches,
The state of this place is really absurd,
But the worst of all is the doggy turd.

This graveyard was once the pride of the East End,
It could really do with a fix and a mend,
To clear up the rubbish, the junk and trash,
And perhaps an injection of lottery cash.

If I had millions of pounds to spare,
One thing I would do and this I will swear,
Is repair all the damage, the destruction would cease,
So the dear departed could rest in peace.

L Brooks

DAYS OUT

Saturday night
Flying high
Kids playing around
Lost and found
Misery
But happiness for the kids
Eyes looking from the TV
Talking
Walking
Drilling mad
And unhappy
See you Sunday
Circumnavity
Irrationality
Insubordinality
Ah!
My head hurts.

Mark Lloyd

IF I COULD BE

If I could be a bee so gay,
I'd hum by night and hum by day
I'd drink the pollen that I could
and do the things a good bee should.

Pamela Coope

YEARNING!

My heart yearns for a lover,
She is so near, yet far,
My love for her shines brighter
Than any heavenly star!
Alas, she loves another
And every time we meet,
A fragment of my broken heart,
Lies shattered at her feet!

A E Garrod

RED

They say the red is rare
and rarely seen.

Not because their shy-snobby
out to lunch, or have become an
old has-been!

No - I don't think so!

The numbers are dwindling
slowly - but I'm afraid it's true.

Why?

Well, at first we didn't have a clue.

Then like a bolt out of the blue,
it hit us like a bright, shining ray.
It's all the fault of its neighbours
that multiplying, pushy, pesky
dull-grey.

Peter de Dee